Garden

City

Also by John Mark Comer

*My Name Is Hope: Anxiety, Depression
and Life after Melancholy*

*Loveology: God. Love. Marriage. Sex.
And the Never-Ending Story of Male and Female*

God Has a Name

Garden

Work, Rest,
and the Art of Being Human.
John Mark Comer.

ZONDERVAN®

City

ZONDERVAN

Garden City
Copyright © 2015 by John Mark Comer

Requests for information should be addressed to:
Zondervan, *3900 Sparks Dr. SE, Grand Rapids, Michigan 49546*

ISBN 978-0-310-33734-8 (softcover)

ISBN 978-0-310-33732-4 (ebook)

Library of Congress Cataloging-in-Publication Data

Comer, John Mark, 1980–
    Garden city : work, rest, and the art of being human / John Mark Comer. —
1 [edition].
        pages   cm
    ISBN 978-0-310-33731-7 (hardcover)
    1. Theological anthropology — Christianity. 2. Vocation — Christianity. 3. Work —
Religious aspects — Christianity. 4. Christian life. I. Title.
BT701.3.C65   2015
248.4 — dc23   2015015500

Published in association with Yates & Yates, www.yates2.com.

Cover design: *Ryan Wesley Peterson*
Interior design: *Ryan Wesley Peterson*
Edited by *Carolyn McCready and Becky Jen*

First printing June 2017 / Printed in the United States of America

24 25 26 27 28 LBC 29 28 27 26 25

In *Garden City* John Mark Comer takes the reader on a journey —
from creation to the final heavenly city. But the journey is
designed to let each of us see where we are to find ourselves
in God's good plan to partner with us in the redemption of
all creation. Smack-dab in the middle of this set of ideas is
Comer's excellent sketch of work, a sketch I find both pastorally
mature and an exhortation to each of us to know that all we do
has value before God. There is in *Garden City* an intoxication
with the Bible's biggest and life-changing ideas.

Scot McKnight, Julius R. Mantey Professor of New
Testament, Northern Seminary

There is an awakening happening in the Western church. We
are rediscovering that God's mission includes all of creation,
not just church work, and he intends for us to be flourishing
people, not just religious disciples. John Mark Comer's book
continues this awakening with accessible insight into forgotten
biblical truths about the importance of our identity as women
and men created in God's image, the value of our vocations in
the world, and a ravishing vision of the beautiful future we are
building with God today. Everyone who reads this book will
see themselves, their work, and their world with new eyes.

Skye Jethani, author of *With*, *Futureville*, and the *With God
Daily Devotional* (WithGodDaily.com)

His writing is informal and infectious, growing on the reader as the topics get more intimate.

Does what we do for work — in an office, factory, kitchen, or studio — matter to God? Is "the Lord's work" relegated to those who receive paychecks from churches and nonprofits? In *Garden City*, John Mark's unique knack for distilling lofty academic concepts into pragmatic, reader-friendly prose focuses on the hugely important and often overlooked inter-connectedness of faith and vocation. Knowing him like we do, it's easy to see his profound desire to know and live the way of Jesus, and to pursue work that matters to God's redemptive plan, poured out on these pages.

The elders of Bridgetown Church

#gardencitybook

If you enjoy the read, please tell your friends.

The path

Genesis 1–2

Then God said, "Let us make mankind in our image, in our likeness, so that they may rule over the fish in the sea and the birds in the sky, over the livestock and all the wild animals, and over all the creatures that move along the ground." So

God created mankind in his own image, in the image of God he created them; male and female he created them. God blessed them and said to them, "Be fruitful and increase in number; fill the earth and subdue it. Rule over the fish in the sea and the birds in the sky and over every living creature that moves on the ground." ... Thus the heavens and the earth were completed in all their vast array. By the seventh day God had finished the work he had been doing; so on the seventh day he rested from all his work. Then God blessed the seventh day and made it holy, because on it he rested from all the work of creating that he had done.... Now the LORD God had planted a garden in the east, in Eden; and there he put the man he had formed. The LORD

God made all kinds of trees grow out of the ground — trees that were pleasing to the eye and good for food. In the middle of the garden were the tree of life and the tree of the knowledge of good and evil. A river watering the garden flowed from Eden; from there it was separated into four headwaters. The name of the first is the Pishon; it winds through the entire land of Havilah, where there is gold. (The gold of that land is good; aromatic resin and onyx are also there.) The name of the second river is the Gihon; it winds through the entire land of Cush. The name of the third river is the Tigris; it runs along the east side of Ashur. And the fourth river is the Euphrates. The LORD God took the man and put him in the Garden of Eden to work it and take care of it.

Welcome to the art of being human

The other day I was out for coffee with my friend Dave.

I live in Portland, which is basically the best city for coffee in the world.[1] Sadly, it's not the best city for sunshine. It rains here. A lot. So we spend a large chunk of the year hibernating in coffee shops, waiting for that strange, yellow object in the sky to re-emerge.

All of which leads me to Dave.

Dave had asked if we could get together and talk about his fight with depression. Unfortunately, I'm a bit of an expert on the subject. My own tangle with depression was brutal and terrifying, but I made it through, and here I am. A better man because of it, oddly enough. I learned a fair bit through my years in the maw of the beast, and I'm always happy to help however I can.[2]

Dave wasn't suicidal or anything, just unhappy. But he had no clue why. He kept saying, I don't get it. I follow Jesus. And I have a great life. Why am I depressed?

My take on depression is that it's more of a symptom than a disease. That something in your life is *causing* the depression.[3] So usually with somebody like Dave I start digging. What's *underneath* the depression? The root under the ground?

Dave was kind enough to put up with my interrogation — Are you sleeping enough? How are you eating? Do you exercise? Talk to me about your prayer life? How's your marriage? I was relentless. But he couldn't think of anything "wrong" with him.

Then I started asking questions about his job.

Do you like what you do?

It's a good job, he said.

Yes, but do you *like* what you do? Do you wake up in the morning with a sense of anticipation? Of excitement for the day ahead?

Well, no, not really.

And for good reason. It turns out that Dave used to be a Navy Seal. Full on. He can hold his breath under water for like three days.[4] After he got out of the Navy, he moved back home to Portland and took over his dad's lighting business. It was a steady income. Great pay. He was able to buy a home and live well. Just one catch — he couldn't care less about lighting. I mean, if you wanted a great deal on a commercial fluorescent, he was your man. But it wasn't *him*. He went from a job pushing his body well past the limit and risking his life every day to a cold metal desk with a laminate top and a computer stuck in Excel.

So I asked Dave one of my favorite questions, If you could do *anything*, what would you do? He started to slide around in his chair. Discomfort was all over his face.

Most of us are too scared to even *think* about that question. The odds of letdown are really high.

In fact, you're probably feeling like Dave right now — questions racing through your mind.

What about the fact that *billions* of people in the world live hand-to-mouth? They're lucky just to survive. Loving what you do is a luxury of the rich.

What about the fact that even here in the US, unless you come from money, it's incredibly hard just to eke out a living? The middle class is disappearing. Millions of Americans are underemployed — working minimum-wage jobs with a master's degree from Stanford. American isn't what it used to be.

What about the fact that *most* people hate what they do? They dread work every day. It's the epitome of toil — exhausting and difficult.

These are all legitimate, intelligent questions, and we'll get into them later. For now, set your anxiety aside. I want you to sit in the discomfort of my question to Dave: "If you could do any-thing ..."

After an awkward silence, David said, Well, I guess I would love to be a police officer.

So I asked the immediate follow-up question: Why don't you just quit? Give it a shot?

He immediately started into a litany of reasons why he couldn't do that — the family business, his father was depending on him, his wife, safety as a dad, and so on. Even though he was a bit nervous, I felt like we were on to something.

At the end of our conversation I just said, Dave, here's what I would do: go home. Talk to your wife and then your dad. Think and pray. Why don't you at least try?

Now, fast-forward about six months. I hadn't seen Dave in a while and never heard back on our conversation (okay, so I'm a lousy friend). But the next time I ran into Dave, he was beaming. It was obvious something had changed.

Turns out, he did it. He quit the family business, and his dad was just fine with it. And he got a job with the local police department. He had to start at the bottom, but for the first time in years, he woke up before his alarm.

Dave was the same guy. Same wife, family, church, city, exercise routine, coffee shop, lawn to mow, dentist.

All that changed was his job. What he got up to *do* every day.

Why is that? How could something as mundane and ordinary as a job change everything for Dave?

I would argue it's because *what we do is central to our humanness.*

What's the first question we usually ask somebody when we meet them? (After we get a name and fumble through a few awkward sentences about the weather.)

"So, what do you *do*?"

Granted, that's likely more of a guy question. Women usually ask, "Are you married? Single? Have any kids?" — questions about relationships.[5]

But they are essentially the same question: What are you giving your life to? When you wake up every morning, what is it
you *do* with your small ration of oxygen?

There's a nasty rumor floating around the church right now,
and it sounds something like this: It's *who you are* that matters,
not *what you do*.

Really? Where do the Scriptures teach *that*?

It's true that some of us look to what we do for our identity and
a sense of self-worth.

I'm a photographer.

I'm a designer.

I'm a pastor.

Currently there's a much-needed backlash against this
unhealthy way of thinking. But be careful that the proverbial
pendulum doesn't bang you over the head. What we do *flows*
from who we are. Both matter.

After all, the vast majority of our lives is spent working.

By working I don't just mean our job or career. Work is way
more than what we get paid for. It's cooking dinner, cleaning

your apartment, washing the car, exercise, running errands — the stuff of everyday life.

And the next largest slice of the pie chart is spent resting.

By resting I don't just mean the ancient ritual of Sabbath, although we'll get into that in depth. I mean sleeping, your day off, time on the couch with a good novel or movie, brunch with your friends, vacation — the stuff we look forward to and savor. The moments when we wish life had a Pause button.

In the church, we often spend the majority of our time teaching people how to live the minority of their lives.[6]

I lead a church, so I'm not criticizing anybody but myself right here. Guilty as charged. I teach people how to read the Scriptures and pray and do God stuff. But how much time do we spend reading the Scriptures every day? A half hour maybe? And how much time do we spend in prayer? I know that's a bit hard to measure, so just take a guess. I set aside an hour every morning to read and pray, but still, that's a tiny fraction of my life.[7]

I mean, it's basic math.

Most of us sleep for about eight hours a day. Then we get up and go to work for another eight hours, if not more. But factor in about an hour for your commute — on your bicycle if you live in my city or on the bus or in your car. Throw in some time to stop for gas or get a cup of coffee. Then it takes about two hours a day to eat and take care of your to-dos. And let's throw in another hour for exercise. So now we're at eight hours a day for rest and twelve hours a day for work. That leaves four hours left in your day.

And we all know where you spend *those* four hours . . .

Netflix.

Seriously, all we have is a few short hours a day for the Scriptures, prayer, church, community, the gospel — all the "spiritual" stuff. And that's if you slay the Netflix dragon and give every spare minute of your spare time to cultivating your spirituality.

Honestly, do any of us live this way?

What I'm getting at is this: in the church we need to talk about *all* of life. What it means to be a disciple of Jesus at church *and* at our job, school, gym, coffee shop, on our day off, when we go shopping or to the theater or on a date, and so on. This means we *have* to talk about work, because it consumes the lion's share of our lives.

All too often there is a massive disconnect between "spiritual life" and *life*. The way of Jesus isn't about detaching from the world and hiding in a mountain cave like somebody stuck in an episode of *Lost*. Jesus was a construction worker, for *decades*, in a village, Nazareth. Then he was a rabbi, or a teacher. His way is about living a seamless, integrated life, where the polarization between the sacred and the secular is gone, and *all* of our life is full immersion in what Jesus called the kingdom of God. But this will never happen unless we recapture a theology of work and rest and the art of being human.

The core question of this book, driving every page forward, is, What does it *mean* to be human?

Put another way, Why do we exist? What are we here for? What's our meaning? Our purpose? Is there any?

Every religion and form of spirituality comes up with some kind of answer to these primal, ancient questions. Because we're all born with this haunting question in the back of our mind.

Now, in the church, we usually give a spiritual-sounding answer. I think of the iconic Westminster Catechism: The chief end of man is to glorify God and enjoy him forever.

Sure. Of course. I mean, who's going to disagree with that? But as you may or may not know, the Scriptures open with a very different kind of answer. One that's a lot more down to earth. Literally.

In *Genesis,* God says,

> Let us make mankind in our image,
> in our likeness, so that they may rule ...

There it is.

Staring us in the face all these years.

Why did God make humanity? "So that they may rule." In Hebrew, the original language, it's even clearer. The text can be translated, "God made human *in order to* rule."[8] You and I were created to rule over the earth. That's our meaning, our purpose — it's *why we exist.*

This language of ruling is a little weird sounding to most of us. I doubt the last time your boss asked what you were doing, you said, Just ruling over my email. We'll get into what ruling is all about soon, but for now, let's just say it's a lot like what we call work.

The mantra of our culture is that we work to live. The American dream — which started out as this brilliant idea that *everybody* should have a shot at a happy life — has devolved over the years into a narcissistic desire to make as much money as possible, in as little time as possible, with as little effort as possible, so that we can get off work and go do *something else.*

What a miserable way to live.

It's striking to me that a number of people I know who made a bunch of money and retired young are unhappy. Grouchy. Cantankerous. Angsty.

It's like they lost something central to who they are.

In *Genesis*'s vision of humanness, we don't work to live; *we live to work*. It flat out says we were *created* to rule — to make something of God's world.

That's why unemployment is so gut-wrenching and depressing for people.

It's why people who hate what they do for a living are discontent — no matter how much money they make.

It's why the elderly or disabled are often unhappy and desperately want to contribute to society.

Because when we stop working, we lose a part of who we are.

And the same is true of rest. When all we do is work and work *and work*, day in, day out, with no space, no margin, we grind our soul down to the bone. We become more machine than human being.

So whoever you are, and whatever it is you do …

College student.

Mom.

Barista.

Engineer.

Librarian.

Artist.

Physicist.

Grocery checker at the local market.

This book is for you.

And this book is for me.

Because this book isn't about how to get ahead in your career or spice up your résumé. The guts of this book are about working, resting, and *living* a full existence. About "spiritual life" invading *all* of life. And about waking up to a God-saturated world.

Let's get into it ...

Kings and queens

Why is it that so many of our cultural stories — in literature and art and film — are about princes and princesses, kings and queens? It's the same story over and over and *over* again … some child, from obscurity and abject poverty, does something heroic and somehow becomes royalty.

Why is that?

I would argue it's because it taps into a visceral part of who we are — a desire we *all* have as human beings, no matter how hard we try to suppress it or ignore it or deny it or mock it, it's *there*.

God put it there.

For some of you, it's under lock and key, just waiting to break out. It's a prince in exile, Rapunzel locked away in a tower.

There's an idea, a crazy dream, an unrealistic desire, a haunting sense deep inside you that you were *made* for something. And it won't go away no matter how hard you try to shove it down the drain.

This book is about getting that part of you *out*.

Maybe you're reading this book and you love your work. Remember that by work, I don't just mean your job or career. Hopefully that, but maybe it's parenting or music or photography or serving at your church or fighting injustice — whatever it is you fill your schedule with and give your heart to. Well done. I hope and pray that after reading this book you love it even more and do it even better.

Maybe you're sitting there right now, at your apartment, the park by your house, or a local coffee shop — and honestly, you *hate* your work. You dread it. It's a means to an end. The end is to get off work and go do something you enjoy.

Or maybe you don't mind your job, and the pay is great, but when you get quiet and you let the whisper deep inside you speak, you know your work isn't ruling over the earth in a life-giving way. What you do — the business or company you work for, the product you make, the service you perform, maybe even your profession itself — isn't creating a garden-like world for humans to thrive in. It's just gas on the fire of materialism or sexualization or rampant Western waste . . .

My hope and prayer — and I'm going to be *really* honest here — is that reading this book makes you take a long, hard look at your life and work, and maybe, just maybe, make a change — a new job, even a new career or a new city or a new end goal in life.

That's a crazy, disturbing thought, so if you're not up for it — put this book down right now.

You have officially been warned.

But my guess is a lot of you are reading this book, and you have no clue what it is you're made for. Maybe you're in school, and you think about it every day, but you don't really know. Or maybe you're thirty, or even forty, and you still feel like you're wandering around like an occupational vagabond. You're still not exactly sure what your "calling" is. Or maybe you're at the halfway point in your life, and everything is changing. Your kids are out of the house or you're tired of your career. You're thinking about doing something totally different. My hope and prayer for you is that this book is a compass, not to show you the way step-by-step, but to point you in the right direction.

So, let's dig in and start where all stories start — in the beginning.

The first story in the Scriptures starts with God working and ends with him resting.

The opening line in the Bible is, "In the beginning God created the heavens and the earth."[1] The phrase "the heavens and the earth" is a Hebrew idiom, very similar to our saying, "from top to bottom." It's a way of saying *everything*.

In the beginning . . .

God created . . .

everything.

But at first this new world is "formless and empty."[2] In the original language it's this poetic phrase — *tohu wabohu*. There's all sorts of controversy about how to best translate *tohu wabohu* into English, but a growing number of scholars vote for "barren and uninhabited." So, there's a world, but it's an alien wasteland.

So for six "days" God is hard at work, forming and filling the earth up with life. And at the end of the week we read, "God saw all that he had made, and it was very good."[3] This is God sitting back after a long, hard week's work, sinking into his chair, and thinking to himself, Not bad. It's God drawing joy from his labor. That sense of satisfaction and fulfillment you get when you're good at what you do and you love it.

Then we read, "By the seventh day God had finished the work he had been doing; so on the seventh day he rested from all his work."[4] Rest here doesn't mean God was tired or worn down. It's an act of delight. God is enjoying the fruit of his labor.

And in between the opening line and the closing paragraph, the narrative is filled with metaphor after metaphor for who God is and what God is like.

God is an artist, a designer, a creative ...

He's an engineer, a builder ...

An ecologist, a zoologist, an expert in horticulture ...

A musician, a poet ...

A king, a shepherd ...

But above all, he's a worker, and a vigorous one at that.

Now, the Scriptures weren't written into a vacuum,[5] they were written into time and space. We don't know exactly where or when *Genesis* was written, but for sure in the ancient Near East, a long, *long* time ago.[6]

Genesis wasn't the only creation story in the ancient world. There were others. Dozens of them. All competing for the top place. One of the most popular was the Enuma Elish from Babylon — the cultural epicenter of antiquity. In it the gods are tired of work and start to complain to Marduk, the king of the gods. He comes up with an ingenious plan to outsource the gods' workload — humanity. This is Marduk's line . . .

> I will establish a savage,
> "Man" shall be his name . . .
> He shall be charged with the service of the gods,
> that they might be at ease.

Most of the other creation myths from around this time have essentially the same basic idea:[7] The gods are tired and worn out. Work is thought of as a burden. It's *beneath* the gods. And so humanity is created as cheap slave labor — to do the work of the gods for them. To give them food and drink from sacrifices at the temple. That way the gods can sit back and "be at ease."

Read over against the other creation myths of the day, *Genesis* is shocking. This God — the one, true Creator God — is nothing like Marduk and his divine friends. He doesn't hate work; in fact, he seems to really enjoy it. And instead of creating humanity to offload all his work because it's beneath him, the story opens with God himself working to create a world *for* humanity, a place for us to experience and enjoy his presence. Humanity isn't created as cheap slave labor to do his bidding, but rather as his co-creators, his partners.

Yes, you heard me right.

We are God's partners.

The language that's used in *Genesis* is the "image of God."

God said, "Let us make mankind in our image, in our likeness, so that they may rule over the fish in the sea and the birds in the sky, over the livestock and all the wild animals, and over all the creatures that move along the ground."

> So God created mankind in his own image,
> in the image of God he created them;
> male and female he created them.[8]

We hear this language all the time, but what does it actually mean? To be made in the image of God?

The word *image* is *selem* in Hebrew, and it can be translated "idol" or "statue." An idol is a visible representation of an invisible being. A statue was put in the temple of every god in the ancient world so the worshiper could see what that god was like.

We are God's statues. His *selem*.

We were put on earth — because the entire cosmos is *this* God's temple — to make visible the invisible God. To show the world what God is like. We are the Creator's representatives to his creation.

But that's just the beginning, there's more ...

The phrase *selem elohim,* meaning "image of god," was used all over the ancient Near East, but not just for anybody — for the king.

For example, Pharaoh was called Amon-Re, or image of Re, after Re, the sun god in the Egyptian pantheon.[9] But it wasn't just an Egyptian thing. All over ancient Mesopotamia, the king was called the image of god. He was seen by the people as quasi-divine, as the god's representative, acting on his behalf, ruling in his place. And his relationship to the god was unique. He knew the divine in a way nobody else could ever hope to. The king was his or her high priest — mediating blessing to the kingdom.[10]

Of course we read this three millennia later and laugh it off as PR, spin, nothing more than the propaganda of an ancient megalomaniac. But this way of thinking was woven into the very fabric of the ancient world.

And the dark underbelly to this way of thinking is obvious and axiomatic: If the king is the image of god, that means the rest of us *aren't.* Remember Marduk? Humanity was created as cheap slave labor. Nothing more than a minimum-wage employee to push around.

The theology of the image of God in *Genesis* was, *and still is,* subversive and stunning. It claims that *all* human beings — not just those of royal blood, not just the oligarchy of society, not just white men — *all* of us are made in the image of God.

This is the democratizing of humanity. We are all kings and queens, and the entire earth is our kingdom.

That's why the very next sentence says, "So that they may *rule*." The seamless connection between "image" and "rule" is explicit in the text.

The word *rule* is *radah* in Hebrew. It can be translated "reign" or "have dominion." It's king language. One Hebrew scholar translated it as "to actively partner with God in taking the world somewhere."

That is a seriously great way to put it.

From the beginning of the story, God has been looking for partners.

The imagery of humanity's relationship to God is *not* of puppets on a string, with God up in heaven playing around. Rather, it's of partners, God's representatives on earth, kings and queens, ruling over his world.

Think about it: God could have made humans from the dust, like he did with Adam, but instead he chose to work through marriage and family.

He could have made food fall from the sky, like he did with manna in the exodus, but instead he chose to work through farming and agriculture and trade.

He could have put Adam and Eve into a city, like he's going to do in the New Jerusalem, but instead he chose to put the proto-humans in the Garden and give them a shot at starting a civilization from scratch.

Why? Because *God is looking for partners*.

And that's a dangerous game for God to play.

In the very next paragraph humans are commanded to "fill the earth and subdue it." This word *subdue* is intriguing. In Hebrew it's *kabash*, where we get the saying, "Put the kibosh on it!"[11] (Come on, that's cool.) It can mean to exploit or enslave or abuse or even to rape. But it can also mean to tame something that's wild, to bring order out of chaos, to bring harmony out of discord. Once again, it's king and queen language.

There are good kings,

and there are bad kings.

There are good monarchs, under whose rule a kingdom thrives — civilization grows and expands, the earth flourishes.

And there are evil tyrants, whose reigns are marked by oppression and injustice — dehumanizing people and stripping bare the soil of the earth.

It all depends on what kind of ruler you have.

In *Genesis* we see both. As the story unfolds, humans do a lot of good. Some of them rule very, very well. They build the first city as the locus point for culture.[12] They invent technology. They write music and come up with the arts.[13] They figure out how to raise livestock.[14] Noah is the first one to plant a vineyard and make wine.[15] On and on it goes ...

But humans also do a lot of bad. After Noah has his vineyard up and running, he gets drunk.[16] Then we read about the first case of incest.[17] A guy named Lamech comes up with a horrific "innovation" — polygamy.[18] And the systematic oppression of women is born. Above all, we read about violence. The first human innovation is fratricide — Cain's murder of his brother Abel.[19]

And what is human history but more of the same?

Human beings are responsible for art, science, medicine, education, the Sistine Chapel, Handel's *Messiah*, New York City, space travel, the novel, photography, and Mexican food — I mean, who doesn't love Mexican food?

But we're also responsible for a world with 27 million slaves, blatant racism, the Holocaust, Hiroshima, the genocide in Rwanda, ISIS, the financial meltdown of 2008, pornography, global warming, the endangered-species list, and don't even get me started on pop music.

So we humans are a mixed bag. We have a great capacity —

more than we know — to rule in a way that is life-giving for the people around us and the place we call home, or to rule in such a way that we exploit the earth itself and rob people of an environment where they can thrive.

This was God's risk. His venture. His experiment.

And this is why Jesus came as a *human*. Think about how weird that is. For millennia God had come in an audible voice or in a cloud on a mountain or in a burning bush or even as a whisper in a cave,[20] but this is a startling twist in God's MO. This time around, he comes as a *human*.

Why?

Because the Creator still hadn't given up on his dream for Adam ...

The writer Paul does this ingenious connect-the-dots between Adam and Jesus. It's easy to miss, even though Paul does it in a couple of places.

In 1 Corinthians 16 he calls Jesus "the last Adam."[21]

In Romans 5, he calls Adam the "advance prototype of the one who would come."[22] Meaning Adam, the first human, was entrusted with the ruling of the world, but he was just a sign-post pointing forward to "the last Adam," the one *true* human who would come and rule the world forever, Jesus.

Which makes Paul's next line all the more interesting:

"For if, by the trespass of the one man, death reigned through that one man, how much more will those who receive God's abundant provision of grace and of the gift of righteousness reign in life through the one man, Jesus Christ!"[23]

This is an unexpected twist. Paul's basic idea is that because of Adam's disobedience, we all die, but because of Jesus' obedience, we all live. But in this statement, he takes it to the next level. Not only do we live, but we "reign in life."

Whoa ... slow this down.

"Reign" is king language. It's *Genesis* language. "Reign" is what we were supposed to do all along, before Adam mucked it all up.

Okay, now we're getting somewhere.

God's original intent was *always* for a human being to rule over the world.[24]

Adam had the first crack at it, and he failed.

If you know the story of the Bible, you know that next God called Abraham and his family to take another shot, but tragically, they failed too.

What is the Old Testament but the story of one ruler after another, trying to do what Adam was supposed to do — rule over the earth in a life-giving way — but failing, often miserably?

Ever read through *1* and *2 Kings*? With each Hebrew king that comes to power, you get your hopes up — maybe, just maybe he'll be the one to fix it all — and then your hopes are dashed, time after time after time. By the end of the Old Testament, you're thinking, *How in the world is God going to fix this mess?*

And it's not just *them*, it's *us*.

I've failed.

So have you.

But where Adam and Abraham and Israel and you and I all failed, Jesus didn't.

He did what Adam was supposed to do but couldn't. What Israel was supposed to do but couldn't. What *we* were supposed to do but couldn't.[25]

That's why immediately after his resurrection he's called "King of Kings" and "Lord of Lords" and "the ruler of the kings of the earth."[26]

Even the closing line in the gospel about how Jesus "was taken up into heaven and he sat at the right hand of God"[27] isn't a statement about Jesus' absence from the world, as much as his presence.

What's he doing at the "right hand of God"?

Ruling over the earth.

And what's the first thing Jesus does with his rule? He shares it with us.

Why? Because *from the beginning of the story God has been looking for partners.*

Is this starting to come full circle for you?

This is what we were made for.

Now, let's take a step back. What does this mean for us today? All this talk about kings and queens is fine, but we don't live in the ancient Near East. And most of us aren't royalty. So what does this mean if you're a server at a restaurant? A full-time mom? A landscape architect? A high school student? A nanny? An anesthesiologist?

Well, a lot.

For starters it means that your work is a core part of your humanness. You are made in the image of a *working* God. God is king over the world, and you're a king, a queen —

royalty — ruling on his behalf. Gathering up the creation's praise and somehow pushing it back to God himself.

When you get up tomorrow morning and go to your job or school or whatever it is you do with your life, you're not just earning money to pay the bills or learning microbiology or raising kids or serving at your local church or nonprofit. You're being *human*. You're ruling over the earth.

Secondly, this means we need to think of work as a *good* thing. When God was done working, he sat back and said, This is really good. That's how we should view our work.

So many people think of work as the curse. I hear it all the time, I hate my job. Work is the curse. But *nothing* could be further from the truth. Work is cursed, yes — more on that later. But work itself is the exact opposite — a *blessing.* And no, that's not a misprint. In the creation story we read, "God *blessed* them and said, 'Be fruitful ... fill the earth ... subdue it ... rule ...'" A blessing in *Genesis* is a weighty, strong thing — it's a gift from the Creator God to generate life, fertility, and well-being. And what is God's blessing over humans? *Work.*

We'll get into what "be fruitful" and "fill the earth" mean in the next chapter, but for now, it's basically the work of building civilization. God's original intent was always for human beings to join him in his seven-day rhythm of work and rest.[28] We need to recapture this stunning vision of humanness.

And then lastly, this means that every human on the planet is bursting with raw, uncut potential.

You are bursting with raw, uncut potential.

You have the blood of royalty in your veins.

So wherever you're at — here's the first takeaway: You're royalty. A king or queen. Made to rule, to subdue. You have a dizzying amount of pent-up potential in you — to do good or to do evil.

What kind of ruler will you be?

You were made to do *good* — to mirror and mimic what God is like to the world. To stand at the interface between the Creator and his creation, implementing God's creative, generous blessing over all the earth and giving voice to the creation's worship.

And if you want to know how to do that, keep reading ...

A place called Delight

Okay, so we're kings and queens. Cool. But for those of us who were born in a suburb in California, what does "ruling" actually look like? You pragmatists are reading this book right now and thinking, Soooo what?

Let's keep going.

We left off in *Genesis* with the poem,

> So God created mankind in his own image,
> in the image of God he created them;
> male and female he created them.[1]

But the author wasn't done. I cut him off. Right after that, we read this:

"God blessed them and said to them, 'Be fruitful and increase in number; fill the earth and subdue it. Rule over the fish in the sea and the birds in the sky and over every living creature that moves on the ground.' "[2]

Theologians call this the "cultural mandate," because it's a command to make culture. Fascinating. Adam and Eve are *commanded* to make culture.

And so are we.

If "image of God" is every human's job title, then the cultural mandate is our job description. It's what we're supposed to actually *do*. How we're supposed to go about this whole ruling gig.

There are two parts to the so-called cultural mandate. The first is, "Be fruitful and increase in number," and the second is "subdue." A word on each . . .

First, "Be fruitful and increase in number." At face value, this just means get married and grow a family. We often skip over the simple reading, but let's sit on it for a minute. Just because it's well-known doesn't mean we understand it.

My wife, Tammy, and I have three kids — Jude, Moses, and Sunday. They are a ton of work and money and time and effort and energy and stress, and they are systematically wrecking our house, *and* they are the best thing that's ever happened to us. And because each one is spilling over with raw, uncut potential, each one is a full-time job. So, for now, Tammy is a full-time mom. When the kids are a bit older, her plan is to go back to school and become a nurse. But she's in no rush. She feels like this is what she was made for.

When it comes to parenting, Tammy and I are partners, in it together. But we each play a unique role. She's free to invest more of her time in what's commonly called parenting — the art of unfolding children.

That said, I *hate* — loathe, detest, despise, and any other acrimonious word my thesaurus can't drum up right now — it when people ask me, Does your wife *work*?

Seriously?

Come on.

It bugs me because there's a subliminal message in there — that parenting doesn't really count as a legitimate career. If you're smart and educated and at all forward thinking, why in the world would you waste the best years of your life on your *children*?

Our culture as a whole, and sadly even the church at times, doesn't have a high view of parenting, at least, not as a career. God's view of the family, however, is over-the-top. To him, it's the first thing on human's job description.

There's a reason why married couples who can't have kids usually feel deep pain and anguish over infertility. One of my best friends has been married for fifteen years; he and his wife have tried everything, but they haven't been able to get pregnant. I watch them grieve the death of a child that hasn't even been born.

My point isn't that you all need to go out and get pregnant pronto, and if you can't, sign up for adoption before you go to bed tonight. I'm not even saying you need to get married. Jesus himself was single and celibate. My point is that for those of you who *are* parents — especially if you parent full-time — what you do is at the focal point of God's vision for the world. Well done. Keep it up.

That said, this command to "be fruitful and increase in number" doesn't *just* mean get married and have kids. It's more than that. After all, why would God *command* it? I'm pretty sure it would just happen. Human beings aren't very good at keeping their pants on, and birth control wasn't exactly easy to come by ten thousand years ago. Why is this part of human's job description? I mean, animals are "fruitful" and "increase in number," but it's not ruling. What gives?

The key is in the next line: "Fill the earth."

The idea here is for Adam and Eve to take their fledgling family and make it into something more — a society. God wants more for Adam and Eve than an ancient version of Swiss Family

Robinson; he wants a civilization. He wants human beings to make babies *and* to make churches, community centers, schools, social services, governments, entire countries. All of this falls under the rubric of "fill the earth."

Which leads to the second part of human's job description: "Subdue it." Meaning, harness the raw, uncut potential of the earth itself. Make something of the world you've been dropped into.

You have a forest — do something with it.

You have a river — make it work for you.

You have metal deep in the earth's crust — get it out.

You have sun and wind and soil and rain — *do something with it*.

Plant crops, build houses, invent solar power, design computers, make music, shape art, come up with technology — *fill the earth and subdue it*.

This word *subdue* seems to indicate there's an inherent wildness to the world. It's untamed. Out of control. In desperate need of ruling.

We have a picture in our head of the antediluvian world as perfect — this dreamy mirage of leisure and opulence. But that's *so not* the picture in *Genesis*. The first thing we read is that the world is *tohu wabohu*. One of my favorite Hebrew scholars translated that line as "wild and like a wasteland."[3] And then the first week is a flurry of activity. God is hard at work, taming the earth into something hospitable for life. Then human is created to rule — to continue the project that God started. To subdue his adolescent world. This is the language of conquest and colonization. To wrestle with the earth and wring profit from its hands.

But once again, that doesn't mean trash the environment, pollute the atmosphere, stockpile nuclear weapons, strip-mine for ore, farm away the topsoil, or any other stupid thing that we've done in the name of "the Bible says." No, there is a very specific *kind* of world we are to make. It's called Eden.

There are actually two creation stories in *Genesis*. Chapter 1 tells the story from thirty thousand feet — it's about the "heavens and the earth." But then chapter 2 zeroes in on a Garden called Eden — a Hebrew word meaning "delight." This spot's address is Delight. Not a bad place to call home. We read this:

"Now no shrub had yet appeared on the earth and no plant had yet sprung up, for the LORD God had not sent rain on the earth and there was no one to work the ground ..."

So the world is incomplete. There's no tree, no bush, no agriculture or irrigation, and no human.

"Then the LORD God formed a man from the dust of the ground

and breathed into his nostrils the breath of life, and the man became a living being."

In Hebrew there's a play on words. *Adam* (the man) is made from the *adamah* (the ground). It's a poetic way of saying that human has a symbiotic relationship with the earth itself. We're made from the dust. Which is why the first human profession was gardening . . .

"Now the LORD God had planted a garden in the East, in Eden . . ."

And . . .

"The LORD God took the man and put him in the Garden of Eden to work it and take care of it."**4**

Let's drill down on two ideas here: *work* it and *take care* of it.

The first word is *abad* in Hebrew, and it basically means work. But that's not the only way it's translated into English. Sometimes it's translated "service." So work is service.

Service to God.

Service to people made in his image — which is everybody.

And, I would argue, service to the earth itself.

But *abad* is also the same word used all over the Hebrew Bible for worship. Interesting. So work and worship aren't two separate ideas. They are connected at the hip. They are two translations of the *same word.*[5] It's tragic that we think of worship as a few songs at church every Sunday. That *is* worship — of course. But in a *Genesis*-shaped worldview — *all* of life is worship.

When you to go work every day, at least if it's Garden kind of work, it's an act of worship to the God who made you.

Now, this text is the first time we actually read the word *work*. Before this, all the language is lofty and conceptual — rule and subdue. But in Eden, it's gritty and earthy. Human is put in the Garden to "work it." Sometimes our picture of the Garden is of Adam and Eve sitting on the beach sipping mai tais, perusing *Vogue*, and working on a tan. But the reality is, even in Paradise, we were *working*.

The next word we need to take a closer look at is *shamar*, and it's even more interesting. It's usually translated as "take care," and that's spot-on. It means to watch over, protect, guard, police, and stand up for the creation.

The first human was an environmentalist. We should be too.

But the imagery isn't of an ecological preserve where we stay on a skinny little path and don't touch anything (although there's a place for that). *Shamar* can be translated "cultivate" or "develop" or "draw out something's potential."

Okay, now we're on to something.

I have to make a confession. I skipped part of the story earlier. It's a bit technical and boring, so I thought you'd just skim it (which I'm sure you would *never* do). But between the line about how God "planted a garden" and how he "put the man in the Garden," there's an entire paragraph. And it's a bit odd sounding — that's why I left it out. Here it is . . .

(Don't even think about skipping this.)

"The LORD God made all kinds of trees grow out of the ground — trees that were pleasing to the eye and good for food. In the middle of the garden were the tree of life and the tree of the knowledge of good and evil.

"A river watering the garden flowed from Eden; from there it was separated into four headwaters. The name of the first is the Pishon; it winds through the entire land of Havilah, where there is gold. (The gold of that land is good; aromatic resin and onyx are also there.) The name of the second river is the Gihon; it winds through the entire land of Cush. The name of the third river is the Tigris; it runs along the east side of Ashur. And the fourth river is the Euphrates.

"The LORD GOD *took the man and put him in the Garden of Eden . . ."*[6]

Have you ever read that paragraph and thought to yourself, *Why is that there?*

I love that parenthetic line — "The gold of that land is good; aromatic resin and onyx are also there."

I used to read that and think, *Who cares?*

But I think I see what it's getting at now.

The author is saying that Eden is made up of *raw materials*. It's spilling over with pent-up potentiality. Everything you need to make a civilization is there; all you have to do is to cultivate it, to draw it out. But that's going to take some work.

I love Tim Keller's definition of work. He puts it this way: work is "rearranging the raw material of God's creation in such a way that it helps the world in general, and people in particular, thrive and flourish."[7]

Bring it.

This rhythm is found in all sorts of work.

When a farmer takes soil and seed and rearranges it into a crop teeming with food for people to eat and enjoy.

When a builder takes a tree and a rock and rearranges it into a home for somebody to sleep and play and make love and relax and *live* in.

When a fashion designer takes fabric and metal and rearranges it into something with shape and beauty and functionality.

When a musician takes a sound and a tone and a melody and rearranges it into something coherent and mesmerizing.

When a graphic designer takes a shape and a color palette and a typeface and rearranges it into something catchy and tasteful.

All of this is the work of cultivation. Of drawing out something's potential. In fact, our word *culture* comes straight from this idea of cultivation. Good culture is the result of even better people hard at work, rearranging the raw stuff of Planet Earth into a place of delight.[8]

So we're not just called to any kind of work. Some work doesn't do this at all. Some work is destructive to the earth, to the human brain, to the economy, to the family, to the developing world. We're called to a very specific kind of work. To make a Garden-like world where image bearers can flourish and thrive, where people can experience and enjoy God's generous love. A kingdom where God's will is done "on earth as it is in heaven," where the glass wall between earth and heaven is so thin and clear and translucent that you don't even remember it's there.

That's the kind of world we're called to make.

After all, we're just supposed to continue what God started in the beginning.

Here's what you have to understand: the Garden was *dynamic*, not *static*. Put another way, creation was a *project*, not a *product*. The Garden was designed to go somewhere.[9] God's vision was for the order and artistry and beauty of Eden to spread out over the whole earth — and human was the one entrusted with that job, to "fill the earth" with the Garden's reality.

When you think of Eden, don't think of a public park with a lawn, a play set, and a flowerbed or two, where God hands Adam a lawnmower and says, Keep it tidy, will ya?

Think of a violent, untamed wilderness teeming with beauty, but no infrastructure, no roads, no bridges, no cities, no civilization, and God says, *Go make a world.*

Adam wasn't a landscape-maintenance employee. He was an explorer, a cartographer, a gardener, a designer, an architect, a builder, an urban planner, a city-maker.

That's why *at the end* of the Bible, when the prophet John sees the future world remade at Jesus' return, he writes about it in the language of Eden. The last two chapters of *Revelation* are dripping with allusion after allusion to the *first* two chapters of the Bible. We read about ...

"The tree of life,"

"The river,"

"No longer will there be any curse,"

"They will reign (or *rule*) for ever and ever."[10]

The writer John is saying that the future is the return to the past. It's the return to Eden. But notice, something has changed. It's not a garden anymore; it's a Garden-like *city*.

Why?

I mean, you would think that if Jesus' agenda is to fix the world gone awry, then the story would end up back where it all started — in Eden, with everybody naked and unashamed. But instead, it's a little different. Actually, it's *a lot* different. It's a Garden-like city called New Jerusalem with walls and gates and streets and dwellings and art and architecture and food and drink and music and *culture*.

Why is that?

Because the Garden was never supposed to stay a garden; *it was always supposed to become a garden city.*

Boom.

I feel like there should be applause or something right now. Or maybe an M83 soundtrack in the background?

Now, to wrap up this chapter, let's drag all this heady language into the here and now. I think this has a shot at reframing how we think about work from the ground up.

The writer Paul has this letter to the Corinthians in the New Testament. In it, he writes about how he and his friend Apollos both played a strategic role in the church. He puts it this way, "I planted the seed, Apollos watered it, but God has been making it grow."[11] Now, planting, watering, growing — this is Eden imagery, and it's likely that any self-respecting first-century Jew would have picked up on the allusion.

And all of Paul's language builds up to this staggering line: "For we are God's coworkers."[12]

This is a provocative metaphor. Most of us think of ourselves as God's employees, not his coworkers. As if we're working *for* God. And there's some truth in that. Paul loves to call himself God's servant. But if we're God's coworkers, that means we're not only working *for* God, we're also working *with* God.

He's back to the imagery of partners.

What's the difference between an employee and a partner?

In one word — ownership.

One of my first jobs was as a barista at this place called Coffee People. It was the anti-Starbucks of the late '90s. This grassroots, Portland-based, locally roasted, stick-it-to-the-man café was the closest thing to third wave before there *was* a third wave. Once in a while I would be sitting there, bored out of my mind, and then all of the sudden twenty or thirty people would all walk in at once.

We called it "the rush."

The rush was an adrenaline junkie's dream. It was hectic, loud, stressful, go-go-go. And it was hard work.

Anybody who's worked in the service industry knows about the rush and knows that employees usually complain and gripe about it. Because if you're an employee, you're only there to get a paycheck, and you get the same pay whether it's busy or slow. You just wanna put in your time and go home.

But if you're a partner, if you have *ownership,* then everything is different. You work the same job, but harder. The same shift, but longer. *And you're on top of the world.* When the door opens and a dozen people tumble in with somewhere to be in a hurry, you think to yourself, *Sweet.*

So what does this have to do with our work? I'm getting to that. Actually, I think we're there ...

When you go to work tomorrow, remember, you're not just a

designer with a clothing label; you're a partner with God, taking the human project forward.

You're not just a mom or dad getting your kids off to school or reading a story before bed; you're living up to God's call on your life to "be fruitful and increase in number."

You're not just a contractor, working long, hard days in the heat and cold to build a house; you're cultivating the earth, drawing out its potential, and reshaping the world into an environment for people to live as God intended.

You're not just a student going to class, or a light-rail operator going to the station, or a software engineer working on a new app, or a chef coming up with a new recipe, or a scientist in his or her lab, or a checker standing in place at a grocery store, or an entrepreneur working out some crazy idea ...

You are a modern day Adam or Eve. This world is what's left of the Garden. And your job is to take all the raw materials that are spread out in front of you, to *work it*, to *take care of it*, to *rule*, to *subdue*, to wrestle, to fight, to explore, and to take the creation project forward as an act of service and worship to the God who made you.

The unearthing
of a calling

There are seven *billion* people on the planet.

7,156,658,777 to be exact.[1]

That's a lot of people. It sounds like we've done a pretty good job with the "be fruitful" bit. But one of the striking things about humanity is how different we all are — unique, diverse, variegated — *different*. No two of us are the same.

This has profound implications for how we bear God's image. We're *all* called to rule/subdue/work/take care of the earth, but we each do that in a unique way. The ecosystem of humanity is complex and multiform and intricate — each of us has a part to play.

Take, for example, the coffee I'm drinking right now. It's really good. A barista made it in the shop below my office. But somebody else built the machine he brewed it in. And somebody *else* built the coffee shop where he works. And somebody *else* started the coffee shop and hired him. But somebody *else* fronted the money for it all. Not to mention the coffee itself — it came from the other side of the world, from a farm in Peru.[2] Somebody had to go there, build a relationship with the farmer, and strike a deal that was fair. But that never would have happened if there weren't people in education and politics and pop culture who were talking about the need for fair trade and how most of the coffee that people drink is dependent on slavery. So somebody — a teacher, a professor, a politician, a celebrity — had to change the way we think about coffee, I mean, slavery ... and then somebody *else* had to go find a farmer ... and then somebody *else* had to ship it all the way to the Northwest of America, and then somebody *else* had to roast it, just for the guy downstairs to pour me a cup of really good coffee for two bucks.

I could keep going about the desk I'm writing on, the laptop I'm typing away at, the light over my head, the clothes on my back, the building I'm in, the streets I walked to get here — and don't even get me started on my chair.

Can you imagine if I tried to make and do everything by myself? It would take me a lifetime just to come up with a sorry excuse for an office.

My point is that civilization isn't a Wild West with every man for himself — it's a web of billions and billions of people all working together for a better world in a spirit of collaboration and interdependency — each one contributing something unique.

Now we're getting into the idea of vocation.

Vocation is one of those old, tired, outdated, overused, cliché, brilliant, stunning, essential, captivating words we swim in all the time but don't really realize how deep it goes.

The word itself is a relative newcomer on the scene. It goes back a few hundred years at most. But the idea is ancient. We get it from the Latin word *vocatio*. Basically the word means "calling."

Your vocation is your calling in life.

Now, the word *vocation* isn't used in the Scriptures, so there's no right way to define it. In this chapter, I'll give you my take.

Let me just say this right off the bat: I believe God "calls" pastors and missionaries, *and* I very much believe that God "calls" bankers and bakers and artists and accountants and stay-at-home moms and teachers and baristas and maybe even used-car salesmen, but I'm not sure. I am sure about baristas though.

In the next chapter we'll get into the sacred/secular divide and how there is no such thing and it was basically made up by men like myself with self-esteem issues. But for now, just know this: calling or vocation or whatever you want to call it isn't limited to "spiritual"-type jobs and careers. It's as wide as humanity itself.

We often think of calling as this mysterious, enigmatic idea. I know lots of people who are waiting around for a calling from God to come in the form of a dream or a vision or a crazy prophet who walks up to them on the sidewalk with fire in his eyes and a word from God — *Go become a rock-climbing instructor.*

And that does happen.

I think of Moses and the burning bush in Sinai or Paul on the road to Damascus.

But what if those stories are in the Scriptures not because they are normative, but because *they are the exception to the rule*? Because for most of us, calling is much more ordinary and normal and low-budget and made-for-TV.

I think a better way to think about calling is as *what God made you to do*. How you're hardwired by God.

I'm a sucker for personality tests — you know those? Myers-Briggs, DISC, StrengthsFinder — I eat that stuff up. It's the art and science of humanness. It's self-discovery — learning who

God made us to be. And they are incredibly helpful. I honestly think that we're more likely to figure out our calling from a four-letter Myers-Briggs label than we are from a burning bush. Although, if I had the option, I would go for the bush every time. But so much of finding your calling is about finding out who you *are* and what you alone can contribute to the world.

The word *vocatio* can also be translated *voice*. Man, that says a lot. Your vocation is your *voice.*

The Quakers have a saying about calling that I love: Let your life speak.

Finding your calling is about finding your voice — what cuts over all the din and drone of the other seven-billion-plus people on earth. The tune and tone that only you can bring to the table.

Calling isn't something you *choose,* like who you marry or what house you buy or what car you buy; it's something you unearth. You excavate. You dig out. And you discover.

We usually ask little kids, What do you want to be when you grow up? I wonder if we're setting them up for failure with that question. Maybe a better question is, Who *are* you? What do you think God made you to do when you grow up?

That, my friends, is the question. Who *are* we? How are we hardwired by our Maker? What is it that God had in mind the day we were born? These are the questions of calling and vocation.

I was brought up in a culture that essentially said, John Mark, you can do anything you put your mind to. If you work hard enough, if you believe in yourself, if you're patient, you can do anything. This is *such* a middle-class-and-above American way to think. Nobody in the developing world would ever talk like that. And if you're a millennial and you came of age during the recession, fewer and fewer of us talk like that either. But still, one of the reasons we're so disillusioned with the economy right now is because, somehow, this idea of "I can be anything I want" is bred into us by our ancestry. And it's not all bad. It gave me the courage to dream and ideate and step out in life.

But it's also dangerous because, sadly, *it's not true.*

I *can't* be anything I want to be, no matter how hard I work or how much I believe in myself.

All I can be is *me.* Who the Creator made John Mark to be.

If we fight the image of God in us — even if we succeed in the short run — it will come back to eat us alive.

If you're an introvert and you go into sales and you're with people ten hours a day — it will suck you dry.

If you're a thinker with a rapacious appetite for learning but you go into manual labor, it's going to drive you insane.

If you're a natural leader and love moving people forward toward a goal but you end up doing research or writing papers for a university or lab, it's only a matter of time until you go nuts.

Now, at some point, we just need to be thankful for a job. The economy is in and out of the tank, and some of us have it pretty tough. And it's also true that Jesus is with us no matter what we do, and what he called "life to the full"[3] isn't dependent on having our dream job. At all. Which is great, since billions of people see work simply as a way to survive. We'll talk more about that later. For now, all I'm saying is what we *do* should grow out of who we *are*.

There's a lot of talk about burnout right now. As a society, we are overworked, tired, stressed out, and frazzled — the digital age is hollowing out our soul. But burnout isn't always the result of giving too much; sometimes it's the result of trying to give something *you don't have to give in the first place.*

You learn this when you try to do something and you fail. Or worse, you succeed but a part of you dies inside.

This just happened to me. The church I lead is part of a family of churches in our city. I used to lead all three. I was responsible for the direction of three churches and three elder teams and a ton of type-A, high-level leaders, a collective staff of ninety-plus, and a host of other stuff. Oh, and I took this job when I was barely *thirty*. I was in meeting after meeting *after meeting,* working my tail off to push this thing forward, and I was *miserable*. I mean, so unhappy I could barely get out of bed in the morning. After about three years of harrowing my soul to the bone, I finally realized that what I was doing was outside of God's calling on my life. I was burnt out because I was trying to be someone I'm not, to give something I don't have. I'm an introvert. I can't change that any more than I can grow three inches or turn my blue eyes green. I *hate* meetings. I wanna be alone with my library and a few close friends.

God's made my calling clear — I'm just a voice. I'm supposed to speak vision to the church, teach the Scriptures, and write a little bit. That's it. That's what I believe God put me on this earth to do. Waking up to this was brutal. Because it was embarrassing. Basically, I failed at my job. I was frustrated; people were frustrated with me. It wasn't working. So I asked the elders at my church if I could quit. They were gracious enough to say yes (maybe they were thinking, *Finally.*) Now I lead just one church, not three. And I share the leadership with an amazing team of people. I can be myself. I make less money, have less clout, have way less to brag about, *and I feel human again*.

We need to learn to embrace our potential *and our limitations*. Because *both* of them are signposts, pointing us forward into God's calling on our life.[4]

Now, let's flip the conversation around from me, to you.

Maybe you're sitting there reading this book and you know exactly what it is you're called to do. Sweet. You're off to the races.

But maybe you're reading this and you don't really have a clue what you're called to. You feel like you're trackless. Visionless. Lost and confused. You would give anything to know.

Or maybe you're somewhere in the middle — you have a sense of what God made you for, but you don't really see it yet, at least not clearly.

In my experience, the best way to find your calling is to start asking questions. Lots of them. As I said before, calling is something you unearth, deep inside you. These are the kinds of questions I would ask ...

What do you love?

What are you passionate about? What makes you angry? Sad? Happy? Energized? What keeps you up at night? Maybe you're quiet — what's that one thing you always like to talk about?

Start there.

It's my question to Dave: If you could do *anything*, what would it be?

Another way to ask this is, What would you do with your life if you didn't get paid and you didn't need the money? Some of you are thinking — sit by the pool? No, *after* you did that for a year and were bored out of your mind. What would you *do* if money wasn't an issue?

For me, I would teach the Scriptures. The art of learning an ancient God-inspired text and then dragging it into our world is enthralling to me. And I would write. I come alive when I write. It's what I love. It's what I feel I was made for. And even though both are hard work, and there are days when I just want to sleep in and watch *Star Wars*, I really do love what I do.

My mentor Gerry's advice to young people is this: Figure out what you love, and then see if you can make a living at it.

The realists out there are scoffing right now. Come on, grow up. And for good reason. A lot of the time we can't do what we love. That's okay. But it's still worth giving it a shot. Other times we can, just in a different way.

My friend Casey wanted to be a career musician *so* bad. His love was the guitar and singing. He's funny and entertaining and a really good songwriter, and he made a pretty decent record, but it just wasn't quite good enough to tour full-time. Oh, and then his wife got pregnant. He needed a job that could take care of a family. So, at first he was all bummed and depressed and emo, but then he had an idea. He started a guitar shop. He makes custom guitars — over-the-top, amazing, high-end, beautiful custom guitars for some of the best guitarists in music. He was able to take his passion — music — and turn it into a living.

Asking this question is a luxury that most of the world doesn't have. If you're born in Uganda, where my daughter is from, you don't think about doing what you love; you think about doing anything you can to survive. But in the West — because of our staggering level of wealth, we have a chance to follow our heart. It's crazy to me that some people don't at least try.

What are you good at? (Oh, and bad at?)

Hopefully the answer to this question will be the same as the last, but not always. How many of us know somebody who wants to sing or play football or design clothing or *whatever*, but they just aren't very good at it?

Growing up, I wanted to be a professional basketball player. I would watch this movie, *Pistol Pete* (anybody?), about this kid who later became an NBA prodigy, and he would dribble around his living room with a blindfold on and do all these crazy drills in his driveway. So I would go out in the front yard and set up cones and dribble around them and do all this stuff.

There was just one problem. I *suck* at basketball. I mean, I'm really, *really* bad at it. It took me a while to figure that out, and then I had to go bury the dream in my backyard, along with my ball and jersey. It was a sad day. But then I found music. And I was pretty good at that. So I started a band. It went pretty well. We made a few records and eventually ended up on a label. But then I realized that teaching the Bible, well, that was something I could really get good at …

It takes time to figure out our gifting. And then years to develop it. Most of us don't really know when we're young. So experiment.

You'll do some things and come alive, and people all around you will say, Wow, you're so good at that. You should do more of it. And then you'll do other things — like basketball — and your ball will shoot off your longboard-of-a-foot and ricochet into a neighbor's window and you'll have to run and hide. I'm just saying. You'll do some things and you *won't* come alive, and people all around you will say, Umm, maybe you should give something *else* a shot.

That's *okay.* Celebrate it. Every time you fail, throw a party — you just took another step forward in learning what you're *not* called to do. It's not failure if you fail at doing something you're not supposed to do. It's success. Because with each success, *and with each so-called failure*, you're getting a clearer sense of your calling.

Even after a few rough years with my church, I have more clarity right now about my calling than I've ever had before. Because I've learned what I'm good at, *and I've learned what I'm bad at.* And the more I embrace both, the freer I become.

There's nothing like that feeling of being *good* at something. Not arrogant or annoying or stuck up, but that Genesis 1 kind of "God saw all he had made and it was very good" feeling. It's that feeling on Friday afternoon when you look back at your workweek and smile.

I'm a perfectionist, which means I'm harder on myself than anybody, and rarely do I feel great about my work, but there are times when I'm up teaching on a Sunday, and right in the middle of it, I'll have this weird out-of-body sensation when I think, *I was made for this.* That's a feeling we should *all* have on a semiregular basis.

What does your world need?

When you look around at your city, your nation, your generation — the world at large — what is it that's missing? What is it that the world needs more of? When you look out at the world, what do you see and do you think, *Somebody needs to fix that?*

Maybe that somebody is you.

Remember *abad*? Work is serving. Often when we talk about vocation and calling, it's a conversation about self-fulfillment. And it's not all bad, but it goes south really fast. We're followers of Jesus. We believe that fulfillment is found in giving our life *away*, not hanging on to it. Jesus was a servant. So are we. So where does the world need people to serve?

This is where the Scriptures' teaching on manual labor is *so* ahead of its time. Paul tells the Thessalonians to "mind your own business and work with your hands."[5] In the ancient Mediterranean, manual labor was looked down on. Digging ditches for the sewer, paving roads for the city, cooking food for the family — this kind of work was done by slaves and servants and the working poor. Historians argue that the Bible is one of the only ancient documents to hold up blue-collar work as an honorable way of life.

Now, hopefully you love what you do — it's not drudgery or mundane survival. It's a calling. The novelist Frederick Buechner put it this way: Work is "the place where your deep gladness and the world's deep hunger meet."[6] That's what you're looking for — the intersection between what you love and what your world needs.

But your calling doesn't need to be glamorous or hip or in style. For civilization to thrive, we need people to pick up the garbage and recycling bins and farm corn and mill lumber and make the beds for the hotel and deliver the mail. This is all good, *honorable*, Adam-and-Eve work.

Does it make the world a more Garden-like place?

Does it contribute to human flourishing? Is it good for the earth? Good for you? Good for your city, your nation, your world? Good for culture? Does it take the raw materials of Planet Earth — metal and wood and wind and words and ideas and $E=mc^2$ — and rearrange them into a place where image bearers can thrive in relationship to God?

Most importantly, is it something that God smiles on? After all, his opinion of your work matters more than anybody else's. After a hard day's labor, can you hear God whisper in your ear, Well done?

There are some kinds of work that *cannot* be a vocation, or a calling from God.

Using your body in a pornographic or sexualized way.

Manipulating first-time home buyers into loans they can't afford.

Siphoning the natural resources of the developing world so the 1 percent can live just a little bit better.

Personally, I don't think being a sniper or a Predator-drone pilot (or any job in the military where killing is the explicit goal) can be a calling. I just don't see any way to reconcile this with

Jesus' teachings on nonviolence: "Love your enemies, do good to those who hate you, bless those who curse you, pray for those who mistreat you."[7]

Whether you agree with that or not, the fact is some work brings life and healing and hope and beauty to the world, while other kinds of work bring violence and theft and poverty and chaos to it.

The only work that can be a vocation or a calling from God is work that harmonizes with Jesus' vision of the kingdom of God.

What about your work/job/career/business/college major/ five-year-plan/dream? Does it *help* humanity? Will it make the world a better place? A more kingdom-like place? A more Eden-like place?

What are the open doors in your life?

You're not on your own in this. At least, not if you're a follower of Jesus. I very much believe that God is with you. He's *involved*. Now, I'm no fatalist. I don't think that everything that happens is from God's hand.[8] I would put it this way: God is involved in your story to the degree that you open up your life to his authorship.

So what's in front of you? What's happening? What's *not* happening? You gotta be careful with that third question because sometimes a closed door is just a timing thing, or it means you need to go knock a little bit louder or maybe even throw your shoulder into it — but hopefully you get what I'm saying. What has God spread out in front of you?

Sometimes a calling is staring us in the face, we just need to make eye contact.

What is God blessing?

I guess this is the follow-up question to the last one. But it's worth asking. Is there an area in your life that God just keeps blessing? You're good and getting better at it, open doors keep coming your way, and it's doing a lot of good?

Now, some people are just really brilliant and gifted and good at a ton of different things. (I wish I was one of them.) All by itself, this question could lead you in the wrong direction. But in the lineup with all these other questions, maybe something jumps out. It's almost like, in that area, everything you touch turns to gold.

It could be God's way of saying, Hot, hotter, *on fire*. This is what you're supposed to do with your life.

Okay, this next one is pivotal . . .

What are people who know you saying?

Sometimes people who love us know us better than we know ourselves. They see who we really are. *Listen* to those people. If you're married, *listen* to your spouse. If you have parents who love you, *listen* to them. If you're in community, *listen* to them. Ask them, What do you see in me? And then honestly listen, no matter what they have to say.

Do people second your desire? And affirm it? Yes, you're on the right track. You're thinking well. I think you would do great at that. Or do they caution you *against* it? I dunno. That could work out bad for you because _____.

Obviously, opinion and bias come in here. (Don't ask me if you should join the military. I have deeply held convictions about followers of Jesus and violence. You can guess what I'm going to say.) But in the words of an ancient Hebrew sage, "In an abundance of counselors there is safety."[9]

Ask people what they think, and then *listen*.

What's the Spirit stirring in your heart?

This is similar to the first question, but a little bit different because sometimes the Spirit will call us to do stuff we *don't* want to do. Honestly, I swore I would *never* become a pastor. I wanted to go into architecture and design, but here I am. Proof that God has a sense of humor.

Is there something stirring in your heart that you feel like you just *have* to do? To let out? To try, whether you succeed or fail. Is there something that you feel like God's put in your head that one day you'll stand in front of your Maker and answer for?

There are all sorts of things that sound fun to me, and I could hopefully make a living doing any number of them — but teaching the Scriptures is the thing I feel like I *have* to do. Maybe that's a bad example because it's spiritual sounding. But it could just as well be designing homes or inventing green building technology or starting a taco stand — anything you feel God is stirring in you.

Maybe the answer to this one is, Nope, nothing. Fine. That's probably most of you. But maybe there is something, and you carry a healthy, sober fear of God about it. If so, whatever that thing is, go do it . . .

I'm not sure how you're feeling right now — excited, scared, confused, frustrated . . .

Maybe as you run your life through this grid, your calling comes into focus.

Remember that for most of us, our sense of calling starts out vague and unclear — more of a feeling and a desire than a five-year plan — but over time it comes into focus. I believe God called me to start a church in Portland at a really young age — late high school. But I had no clue how it would work or what I would actually do. At thirty-three I'm just now starting to figure out who I am, what I'm passionate about, good at, bad at, wired for, and what God's spread in front of me to do. And I started this process when I was a teenager. For most of us, our calling or vocation won't become clear until our thirties. And that's okay.

If you're in that spot of curiosity or confusion, here's what I would say . . .

Listen for God's voice. Ask him to help you discover your calling. Most of us don't get the burning-bush experience, but some of us do. Ask for it. Get alone, fast, pray, take a retreat, go camping all by yourself, rent a room at a monastery — and listen. Just remember that you have to be quiet to hear.

Parker Palmer, in his masterpiece of a book on vocation, writes this:

"The soul is like a wild animal — tough, resilient, savvy, self-sufficient, and yet exceedingly shy. If we want to see a wild animal, the last thing we should do is to go crashing through the woods, shouting for the creature to come out. But if we are willing to walk quietly into the woods and sit silently for an hour or two at the base of a tree, the creature we are waiting for may well emerge, and out of the corner of an eye we will catch a glimpse of the precious wildness we seek."[10]

And bring other people into the journey. Don't go at it alone. Get your mentor, mom, dad, uncle, roommate, professor, boss, friends — people who know and love you — to take the journey with you.

And then just start living. Follow your heart. Don't be afraid to try stuff. Don't take failure too seriously. For that matter, don't take success too seriously either.

And know that jobs and careers and roles come and go — but calling, at least in the sense I'm writing about it — stays the same through life.

The other day I did a radio interview for my last book. I walked into the station and this guy from my church was there. We'd never had a decent conversation, so I started to ask about his story. He started out as a church planter; then he worked for a clothing company as a retail manager, and now he's in radio ad sales. Talk about three radically disparate jobs! But he said the most insightful thing: Really, they're are all the same. It's people. I love people. And I love getting them excited about something new. That's what God made me to do.

Brilliant.

This happens to *lots* of people. My wife, Tammy, for example. She knows that her job will change halfway through her life. After the kids are older and in school, she'll do something else. Like I said before, she wants to become a nurse. She wants to work in rehabilitation with people after injury. Because her calling is broader than mothering — she feels that God made her to help unfold people into the fullest version of themselves. Right now she does that as a mother with our three kids; in the future, it looks like she'll do that as a nurse. Two totally different jobs, *but it's the exact same calling*.

Here's what I'm saying . . .

If God made you to paint, then go paint.

If God made you to nurture and teach and unfold children, then go do that.

If God made you to engineer bridges, then get to work.

If God made you to teach philosophy, then we need you. Go to school. Get letters after your name. Take the long view. And shape the thinking of tomorrow's world.

Because whatever it is that you're called to do — write a symphony, run a landscaping company, invent hydropower, create a vaccine for HIV/AIDS, start a sandwich shop, teach English literature at Yale, come up with really good vegan ice cream — whatever it is — if you *don't* do it, not only do you rob yourself of the life God's called you to live, but you rob *the rest of us*. We need you to be you.

Don't sell us short. Give us all you got.

Everything is spiritual

So, you have a calling. There's someone God made you to be. Something God made you to do. All you have to do is dig it out from under the rubble of your fear and insecurity and upbringing and culture and consciousness. It's there. Waiting to be found.

But I know what some of you are thinking, Really? I know that God calls people to church stuff, but I'm an IT specialist for a cell-phone company — how is that a calling from God?

To get to a robust, deep, rich, charged theology of work, and for that matter, rest, we have to cross the chasm that is the sacred/secular divide.

And I forewarn you; it is a deep, wide, ominous chasm. So put your boots on …

The sacred/secular divide is this erroneous idea that some things are sacred or spiritual, and they matter to God; but other things are secular or physical, and by implication, they *don't* matter to God, at least, not all that much.

The problem with this widespread, ubiquitous, domineering, destructive way of thinking is that, well, by this definition, *most* of life is secular.

The sacred stuff is a dinky slice of the pie — going to church, praying, reading the Scriptures, evangelism. What is that, 5 percent of our lives? Max? If you're really "spiritual"?

Most of life — the other 95 percent — is spent grocery shopping or walking the dog or cutting your toenails or reading at the park or doing yoga with your wife or eating a burrito and then feeling bloated afterward — but less so if you just finished doing yoga.

This is the stuff of everyday life.

And so most of us feel a little bit frustrated because we think that what we *do* every day — our work and our rest — how we play and unwind and enjoy God's world — is meaningless and pointless and ephemeral and doesn't really matter in the grand scheme of heaven and hell and eternal life because it's not sacred.

So much of life is just mundane. There's nothing glamorous

about it. We don't feel like we're changing the world; we're changing diapers or answering emails or tweaking an Excel spreadsheet. So we feel frustrated, or maybe even empty and aimless, because every night as we lie in bed, we think, *Does any of this matter?*

Or we feel a twinge of guilt because even though our job as an IT specialist isn't sacred, we really enjoy it and are proud of what we do. And every time we come home from work and drink a glass of really good wine or watch a great film or eat a delicious meal, we feel this nagging sense of shame because we enjoy it *so* much — it feels good and right and earthy and *human* — but it's not "spiritual."

This entire paradigm of the sacred and the so-called secular is seriously out of whack. And not only is it untrue, but it's also dangerous. Let me make my point . . .

To start off, let's talk about the word *spiritual.* It's one of those words we use all the time, but as a wise Spaniard with a sweet mustache once said, "I don't think it means what you think it means."[1]

Did you know there's no word for *spiritual* in the Hebrew language?

Hebrew is the language of the first three quarters of the Bible — what we call the Old Testament.

Look up the word *spiritual* in *Genesis* to *Malachi* — the Bible used by Jesus.

It's

not

there.

Why? Because in a Hebrew worldview, *all of life is spiritual*.

Have you ever read that crazy book *Leviticus*? You really should. It's in a part of the Old Testament called the Torah, a Hebrew word meaning "teaching" or "law."

And there are laws — I mean teachings — about every facet of life.

Laws about how to purify yourself for the temple, how to make a sacrifice, how to wash your hands *before* you make a sacrifice, what kind of animal to sacrifice if you have money, and what kind of animal to sacrifice if you're poor. Laws about atonement and worship and justice and mercy …

and

there are laws about skin disease — that nasty, red, itchy spot on your left foot — and what kind of material to make your clothes with and what to do if there's mold in your kitchen (does anybody *not* have mold in their kitchen?) and a woman's time of the month and wet dreams and what to do if your donkey falls into a ditch on the Sabbath and government and economics and social justice and just about everything you can think of.

Why?

Why would God put all that — hundreds *and hundreds* of laws — in the Bible? After all, isn't the Bible supposed to be sacred?

And it's not just that athlete's foot and women's menstruation and erectile dysfunction and taxation and economic theory made it into the Bible, it's that there are *laws* about them. Teachings about how to do or not do them. There's a specific way that the Creator wants us to navigate all this unspiritual, secular, run-of-the-mill stuff.

It's almost like it *matters*.

Even when you get to the New Testament, the word *spiritual* is really only used by Paul. In his writings it means "animated by the Holy Spirit." And for Paul, every facet of our life should be spiritual.[2] I think if you had asked Jesus about his spiritual life, he would have looked at you very confused. My guess is he would have asked, What do you mean by my spiritual life? You mean my *life*? All of my life is spiritual.

Jesus didn't buy into sacred/secular thinking. Not one bit. To him, the God he called Father is as close as the air up against our skin. To him, life is a seamless, integrated, holistic experience where the sacred is all around us. And for Jesus and his way, God wants to be involved in every square inch of our lives.

Because everything is spiritual.[3]

Everything matters to God.

How did we get from Jesus and his God-saturated world to this flat, anemic, two-dimensional way of thinking?

Well, how about a little bit of history? Don't worry, it won't take long. But one of the reasons the sacred/secular divide is so deeply embedded into Western European consciousness is because it's been around for a long, long time.

It's at least as old as Plato and the early Greek philosophers, if not older. Plato — whose fingerprints are all over Western culture — used this dichotomy of a spiritual world and physical world, as if they were two separate places. His goal was to get from one to the other. And over time, this worldview sunk into the church.

It took a while. After all, the early followers of Jesus were mostly Jewish. They were rooted in a *Genesis*-shaped worldview — where Planet Earth, with all its problems and issues, was good at its core, and, in spite of all its glorious imperfections, it was home. The great Jewish hope wasn't to die and go *somewhere else* — for your body to biodegrade and your soul to float off to some spiritual world called heaven in the sky.[4] The hope was of resurrection — bodily, corporeal, flesh-and-blood, dirt-under-your-fingernails resurrection. For the Creator to do his healing, saving work *right here on earth*.

As the Messiah himself said, "Your kingdom come, your will be done, on *earth* as it is in heaven."

This was the hope of Jesus and Peter and Paul and the count-less men and women who first called Jesus "Lord."

But as the church spread out from Jerusalem to cities like Philippi and Corinth and then Athens itself — Plato's home-town — and as Gentiles (non-Jewish people, born into a very different worldview) started to join the church, over the years, the tide turned, and platonic, dualistic, sacred/secular thinking started to infiltrate and infect the ethos of Jesus' people.

It hit a zenith in the Middle Ages when the church was flat-out teaching that all work outside of the church was secular. No matter how Garden-like it was. In fact, the word *calling* was only used for church work. The mentality was, if you want to do something that really matters, something for the kingdom, become a priest or a nun or a monk or a theologian. The only other option is to work hard all day at some job you think is inconsequential, so you can get off work and go "serve the Lord."

And so the cosmic, gargantuan 24/7 kingdom of God was shrunk down to a few hundred people singing songs in a nice building for an hour every weekend.[5]

Then a few hundred years ago there was this whole movement of people who started thinking radical, subversive, freeing, beautifully new — or actually, really *old* thoughts — about God and Jesus and the church and what it means to be human. They called themselves the Reformers. Their agenda was to reform the church from the inside out. And they went to *war* with sacred/secular ideology.

They came up with this provocative and *dangerous* idea they called "the priesthood of all believers." They would quote the writer Peter: "You are a chosen people, a royal priesthood."[6] And then turn around and say shocking things like, *You are a chosen people, a royal priesthood.*[7]

Keep in mind, this was sixteenth-century Europe. There already *were* priests — the guys who worked for the church. They and they alone could mediate on behalf of the Creator to the creation and transport life from God to his people.

But the Reformers — this scrappy kingdom insurgency — said, No, we're *all* priests.

You're a farmer? Sure, *and* you're a priest.

You're a law professor, and you're a priest.

You're a student at community college, and you're a priest.

You mediate between the Creator and the creation. You're his representative. You pass his blessing on to people who know him and to others who don't.

And you're *called.* What you do matters to God a whole lot.

Because it's your ministry.

I have a love-hate relationship with the word *ministry*, which basically means I hate it. I work for a church, and so people ask me all the time, What's it like to be in full-time ministry? or When did you know you were called to ministry? I'm a bit sarcastic and I get annoyed way too easily, so sometimes I crack, When did *you* know *you* were called to ministry?

But I'm a preschool teacher.

So?

All the word *ministry* means is "service."[8] Your ministry is your service — it's the part you play, the slot you fill, the place you do your thing to work for a Garden-like world.

The phrase "full-time ministry" is taboo at our church. Whenever somebody new comes on staff they inevitably let it slip, and I laugh as our team sets them straight. Don't worry; we're nice about it, but we're definitely the language police.

Because if people who work for a church are in "full-time ministry," what does that make everybody *else*? Part-time ministry? Volunteer, pro bono, amateur, wannabe ministry? Not in ministry at all?

And don't even get me started on the word *lay* ...

Remember, all the word *ministry* means is *serving.* We're all serving. We're all in ministry. Some of us, like myself, are serving inside the church, which is great. But the vast majority of you are serving *outside* the church — as a paramedic or a landscape architect or a designer for Google or a hunting guide or a surf instructor or a radiologist or a parking-lot attendant — but that doesn't necessarily mean you're serving outside the kingdom. And it definitely doesn't mean that what you do isn't spiritual or that it doesn't matter to God.

This is why we have to go to war with sacred/secular ideology — because it essentially compartmentalizes God. We have our God box and then our work box and our rest box and our diet-and-exercise box and our entertainment box and our money box — and we cut our life up into tiny little pieces. And in all the masochism, God becomes a line item in our budget, a time slot in our daily routine, a building we go to every Sunday for a few hours. God is effectively shut *out* of the bulk of our lives.

This is disastrous for living the God-saturated, full-immersion, you-can't-swim-to-the-bottom kind of life that Jesus wants for all of us. And if you live this way, then over time it's easy to end up at one of two extremes.

Some people think of themselves as followers of Jesus, *but only in the church*. So at church, they're all-in. They take notes from the sermon and volunteer in the kids' wing and show up for the quarterly justice project. Maybe they even tithe. But when they go to work or the car dealership or the movie theater, they are just like everybody else.

They shop and spend and consume and get sucked into the same old tired uninteresting orbit of more, more, more like everyone else.

They overwork and get burned out and unhealthy like everybody else.

If they're in business, they do business just like everybody else. Chasing after the bottom line no matter what it takes.

If they work in marketing, they sell stuff the same way as everybody else in the business.

This is true of good people — really, really good people — who love Jesus deeply. We see this in people who want to make a ton of money and give it all away for the kingdom — to church planting or evangelism or children in the developing world or fighting malaria in sub-Saharan Africa. And this is *great*. I'm all for it. Obviously. But only if what you actually do for a living is just as good and redemptive and beautiful. It doesn't matter if you make a million dollars and give away 90 percent of it if you made that money doing something cheap or ugly or sketchy or greedy or wasteful or harmful to the earth.

What you do *for* work matters just as much as, if not more than, what you do with the money you make *from* your work.

But then, on the other side of the room, a lot of people think their work has to be overtly Christian.

So if they are a musician, it has to be Christian music.

If they are a teacher, it has to be at a Christian school.

If they start a business, it has to have an ichthus in the logo, or at least on the business card.

And that's not all bad. Some of it's really inspiring. But if *all* of us lived this way, well, it could get really unhealthy . . .

We could end up in a world where the church is a kind of cultural ghetto — a relic from the past, where we used to be known for stunning art and genre-bending architecture and pushing the edge of science and rethinking economic theory, but now we're known for really bad music and cheesy design and parody T-shirts and an odd tribal dialect that nobody else really understands — and the world would just kind of move on without us — maybe even mock us or laugh us off as stupid and then start to shape a totally different kind of culture *without* us …

Man, that would be really lame.

I've heard it said that *"Christian* is a great noun and a poor adjective."[9]

There is no such thing as Christian music, because a melody can't be a Christian, only a songwriter can.

There's no such thing as Christian art, because a canvas can't be filled with the Spirit of the living God, only a painter can.

And obviously there's no such thing as a Christian plumbing business — a business can't be Christian any more than a pipe or a sink or a toilet or a showerhead can. Only a plumber can follow Jesus. And he (or she) can do business in a way that is an outworking of Jesus' kingdom vision, and in that sense the business is Christian, but that's all.

We see this in people who have a great job and are maybe even doing something really good for the world, but they feel like it's not good enough. They want to do something "that matters." So they quit and go to work for a nonprofit or a church. And that's not all bad — we all know that some work *does* matter more than others. What's sad is when people think that working at a nonprofit is spiritual and for-profit work *isn't*. As if "to really serve Jesus" you have to work for a church.

I just took a quick break to walk down to the coffee shop in my building and have coffee with my friend Joe. Joe works for Apple. Lots of people think that my job is more spiritual than Joe's job. After all, I'm writing a book about work and rest and what it all has to do with *God*. But here's the thing: I'm writing it *on a computer.* I couldn't do what I do if Joe didn't get up every morning and go to his job.

The "whose job is more important" game gets really old, really fast.

We need to remember that work — all by itself, for its *own* sake is good. So if you're the IT specialist at a cell-phone company and you can repurpose your skill set to fight injustice or end world hunger or make the name of Jesus famous — fantastic. Go do it. As long as you know that just being an IT specialist is enough. What you're doing matters. You make it possible — along with the tens of thousands of other people who work for your company — for people to pick up a phone and call the people they love, anywhere in the world, anytime of day. That, my friend, is Garden work. What you do is a gift to the rest of us. Thank you for serving.

Maybe right now you're thinking, Yeah, *but* Jesus' marching orders were to make disciples, not troubleshoot IT problems for Comcast.

True, but a number of scholars point out the parallel between the cultural mandate in Genesis 1 ("Be fruitful and increase in number; fill the earth and subdue it.") and the so-called Great Commission in Matthew 28 ("Go and make disciples of all nations.").

They argue Jesus is rephrasing the cultural mandate in light of human sin in exile from Eden, and in light of his in-breaking kingdom.

If that's right (and I think it is), then as followers of Jesus we have a dual vocation. Not one, but two callings.

The original calling — to rule over the earth. To make culture.

And a new calling — to make disciples. To help people come back into relationship with the Creator, *so that they can rule* over the creation. Not just so they can get forgiveness and go to heaven when they die. But so that they can *come back* from heaven and rule over the earth as they were always supposed to (more on that toward the end of the book).

So.

If you're the IT guy, when you go to work on Monday morning, you have not one, but two callings. First, you're called to be a really good IT guy. To make your company's computer systems sing. In doing so, you're working for Eden all over again. Well done.

But you're *also* called to make disciples. To tell people about your Rabbi Jesus. And to live in such a way that people ask questions, not just about IT, but about life, meaning, purpose, joy, peace, community, hope, *why you're a little bit different*. And through that, hopefully you get to invite people to become disciples of Jesus, and follow him into his work of culture making.

The new calling to make disciples does not negate or cancel out the original calling to create culture. It's a both/and. A dual vocation.

Now, the church — mine included — has usually focused *way* more on the calling to make disciples than the calling to create culture. And that's not all bad. I very much believe that the calling to make disciples is front and center.

But we have *got* to do both.

It's easy to forget that Jesus was a builder, or a carpenter. Actually the word used in Greek is *tekton*, and it just means "worker." Jesus lived in the north of Israel in a village called Nazareth. I've been there. There aren't any trees for miles. Everything in Jesus' hometown was made out of black basalt rock. Occasionally you would make a door or stool out of wood, but that was only if you had enough money. The imagery of Jesus in the workshop crafting a table is very unlikely. The odds are he was closer to what we call a construction worker. Strong, burly, tough, hard-working. Either way, he was a *tekton* for *decades*. And if working an ordinary, nonglamorous "secular" job wasn't beneath the embodiment of the Creator himself, why would it be below us?

And it wasn't just Jesus.

Paul, for example, worked as an artisan — a tentmaker — all through his years as a church planter. At one point, he said to his friends, "We worked night and day in order not to be a burden to anyone while we preached the gospel of God to you."[10] Paul didn't see his job as a distraction from his calling to the kingdom, but as a vital part of it. If tent making wasn't beneath the most prolific author in the New Testament, why wouldn't it be good enough for us?

Here's what I'm getting at: If you're a construction worker or a plumber or a teacher or a dental hygienist, you're not a Christian construction worker or a Christian plumber or a Christian whatever.

You're a Christian — a follower of Jesus the Messiah and the Lord of the world.

And you're a dental hygienist. Or a professional football player. Or a *you fill in the blank*.

So do your work — whatever it is — as a follower of Jesus. Because there are no compartments! *Everything* matters to God. The way of Jesus should permeate and influence and shape every facet of your life.

Maybe that means you'll leverage your small business to work for justice and mercy — you'll hire people from the local rescue mission and give away half your profits to low-income school-mentorship programs, and you'll make sure your product is sustainable for the environment and does something for the local economy.

But maybe it just means that you'll show up for your job as an accountant, and you'll do your job really, *really* well, and the world will be a better, more Garden-like place because of it. And every day when you show up for work, you'll embody the way of Jesus, so that your boss, your coworkers, your con-tractors, and your clients will all get a glimpse of what Jesus' way is all about and, hopefully, an invitation to join in.

You need to know that's *enough*. In fact, it's more than enough. It's beautiful.

Some of you are reading this book and waking up to the realization that what you do for a living isn't your calling. It's not what God hardwired you for. And it's not contributing to human flourishing. You need to quit your job or change your major or move to the other side of the world and do what God's put in your heart.

Have at it.

But my hope and prayer is that most of you are starting to realize that what you do for a living *is* a calling and that it matters more than you know. Even if it has absolutely nothing to do with the church, it still has theology and weight and backing and *umph* to it.

Because we live in a world with no compartments.

For those who are spiritual — who are filled with the active, dynamic Spirit of God himself — the line between heaven and earth is thin at best. The sacred is never far away.

And your job, your career, or whatever it is you do all day long, isn't something outside of Jesus' calling on your life — *it's right at the center of it.*

Kavod

I got up early this morning to watch the sunrise. It was really something. A little cloudy, just enough to make it interesting, but no rain. The sun was waking up with a kaleidoscope of yellow, orange, pink, and red — like explosions in the sky.

It does something to you.

When you're sitting there, breathing it all in. It wakes up some dormant gene deep inside your being, some ancient, primal part of you that's been in hiding. It taps into this deep well of gratitude and wonder and mystery. All of a sudden God feels so real, so close, so *good*. And you have this overwhelming sense of peace and hope and maybe even optimism, this sense that it's not really as bad as you think and somehow it's all going to be okay.

Man, I should get up early more often.

But then the other day I got the *exact same* feeling, only it wasn't from a sunrise — it was from a piece of furniture in my living room. Maybe that's weird to you, but I have this thing for architecture and design. If I wasn't teaching or writing, that's what I would do. And I know just enough about furniture design (from a few embarrassing attempts at it) to know how challenging it is. The level of precision is punishing. It's a craft in the truest sense of the word. Anyway, this piece was a credenza that I just ordered from a designer in the Midwest.[1] It's all custom, one of a kind. Solid walnut, quarter sawn, so it gets that nice smooth texture, with just a little oil on top, no stain. And the craftsmanship is top-drawer. Whenever I stop and look at it, I get this instantaneous feeling of gratitude, almost like spontaneous combustion. My visceral, gut reaction is, *Thank you, God, for being* this *good.* I just can't help but see the God behind the tree-turned-credenza and the image bearer who made it. I found out later that Matt, the craftsman, is a follower of Jesus, but at the time I had no idea. Even though it's just a piece of furniture — a hunk of wood in my house — all of a sudden, I'm transported into an awareness of God himself, all around me.

Maybe for you it's not design; it's a really good meal or a concert or laughing around a table with friends on a warm summer night — but there are moments of awareness. When all of a sudden we become acutely aware of the Creator's realness, nearness, and goodness.

What *is* that?

I think it's what the Scripture writers call "God's glory."

A lot of people think of God's glory as his fame or celebrity status. As if glory is how many Twitter followers Jesus has. And while I'm sure Jesus would have a lot of Twitter followers, I think that's missing the point.

In Hebrew the word for "glory" is *kavod*. Literally it means "weighty" or "heavy."

So God's glory is his weight? His heaviness?

The idea behind *kavod* is God's *significance*. He's weighty, as in *important*. There's something about this God that we need to stand in awe of. And all through the Scriptures, God's glory is about two things:

Presence

and beauty.

God's *kavod* was in the temple in Jerusalem, which was at the center of Israel's faith, a portal into heaven itself. A cloud would fill the temple from top to bottom, and it was called the *kavod YHWH*, or the "glory of the LORD."

There's a story in *2 Chronicles* in which King Solomon and all Israel come together to dedicate the temple to God. Tens of thousands of people had spent seven *years* working on it — crafting it into an architectural masterpiece. Solomon gives this amazing prayer, offering it up to God, and then, "When Solomon finished praying, fire came down from heaven and consumed the burnt offering and the sacrifices, and *the glory of the LORD* filled the temple. The priests could not enter the temple of the LORD because *the glory of the LORD* filled it."

And when everybody saw God's glory, they fell face down and "they worshiped and gave thanks to the LORD, saying, 'He is good; his love endures forever.' "[2]

God's *kavod* here isn't his fame; it's his presence — the fact that he was *there*, not far away, but close. Heaven and earth were wed, if only for a moment. And it's his beauty — this staggering sense of how good he really is.

After the people see God's *kavod*, what's the response? The exact same response as when I wake up to the sunrise or walk by my credenza — worship and gratitude for *who God is* and *what God is like.*

The reality is that God's *kavod* is everywhere.

It was in the temple, in a thick, impenetrable cloud, but then in the Psalms we read, "The heavens declare the glory of God; the skies proclaim the work of his hands."[3] God's glory is in every square inch of this universe. God's presence and beauty are all over the place.

So, God's *kavod* is in the temple, and it's in Orion's belt and the Sierra Nevada mountains and the park down the street from my house.

Or to drag it into our day and age, God's *kavod* is at church on Sunday when we come together to worship, and it's at the beach that afternoon when we drive over to watch the sun go down.

Of course God's glory is thicker in some places than others. There was something categorically different about the cloud in the temple, but *kavod* is everywhere. You can't limit it or contain it or schedule it or pigeonhole it or brand it or claim it or control it or run from it. All you can do is close your eyes and live blind; *or* open your eyes and end up face down on the floor.

It was the prophet Habakkuk who said that we're heading toward a world where "the earth will be filled with the knowledge of the glory of the LORD as the waters cover the sea."[4] So right now, not everybody knows about God's *kavod*; some people are blind and oblivious, but in the near future, everybody will know about it. Because the awareness of God's *kavod* will fill the earth like the waters cover the sea.

Now, in the meantime, what does all this talk about glory have to do with work, rest, and humanness?

Glad you asked.

One of the most jarring commands in the New Testament is from the writer Paul:

"Whether you eat or drink or whatever you do, do it all for the glory of God."[5]

We live in a time of overlap between the ages. What one theologian called "the time between the times."[6] Because so many people are blind to God's glory, we, as God's people, are to live in such a way that people start to see God's presence and beauty. But notice Paul's examples. "Whether you eat or drink ..." What could be more ordinary and humdrum than eating and drinking? And then Paul says, *or whatever you do.* Wow, so no matter what it is we do — *everything* — the most mundane, unimportant stuff in our life, should be "for the glory of God."

So the question is, how do we glorify God with all of our lives, not just the overtly "spiritual" stuff? But with everything we do — all the way down to eating and drinking?

For some people, it's an easy answer. If you're a pastor or a "missionary"[7] or a parent or an artist or you work for a faith-based nonprofit — somewhere you can openly talk about Jesus. Then it's clear.

But what if you're an executive assistant at an attorney's office? Or a mechanic for your local Toyota dealership? Or a congressperson in the House of Representatives? Or a toll booth operator? Or an insurance broker? How do you glorify God with your life's work?

My brother-in-law Stephen Kenn is a designer. He and my sister live in downtown LA in a loft — not a fake million-dollar brand-new glass-and-steel "loft" in a new part of town. A *real* loft — in a former warehouse, with a garage door for an entrance, concrete flooring, one window with bars over it, some ladies in extremely short skirts on the street corner outside, oh, and you have to be a "full-time artist" just to rent a space there.

Steve makes really great stuff. He had a jeans company for years, now he's doing furniture and bags. Top-of-the-line, all-leather, very stylish, and they are all made within two square miles in LA.[8] Steve also loves Jesus. Very much. He's one of the most Jesus-like guys I know.

The question that Steve has to wrestle with — that we *all* have to wrestle with in our own way — is, how does he glorify God with *bags*?

Does he burn the name *Jesus* into the leather? Or shape the strap like a cross? Or sew John 3v16 into the lining? Or stuff a paperback version of the gospel of Mark in the pocket?

Or …

does he just make a really, really nice bag?

How do any of us glorify God with our work if it's not overtly Christian?

Well, here's my take: we're the image of God, remember? Our job is to make the invisible God visible — to mirror and mimic what he is like to the world. We can glorify God by doing our work in such a way that we make the invisible God visible by *what we do* and *how we do it*.

Let's take each one in turn.

First off, by *what* we do ...

The Anglican writer John Stott said the kind of work we're called to is, "The expenditure of energy (manual or mental or both) in the service of others, which brings fulfillment to the worker, benefit to the community, and glory to God."[9]

Most of us get the first part of that definition: "Fulfillment to the worker" — Ideally, your work should be a vocation, a calling, work that you feel God made you to do and that you love. And a lot of us get the second part: "Benefit to the community" — it should make the world into a more Garden-like place. But what about "glory to God"? How do we do *that*?

Well, if God's glory is his *presence* and *beauty*, then, as I see it, we glorify God by reshaping the raw materials of the world in such a way that, *for those with eyes to see*, God's presence and beauty are made visible.

When we see a piece of art, we see *behind* the art and get a glimpse of what the artist is like.

When we hear a piece of music, we hear *behind* the music and get a faint idea of what the composer is like.

In the same way, when we see creation, we see *behind* the creation and get a picture of what the Creator is like.

In *Romans* we read, "Since the creation of the world God's invisible qualities — his eternal power and divine nature — have been clearly seen, being understood from what has been made, so that people are without excuse."[10]

Theologians call this general revelation. It's the idea that every-body everywhere has at least some revelation of who God is and what he's like, just by living in his world. *Romans* is just picking up on the Hebrew poetry we read earlier: "The heav-ens speak of the glory of God."[11]

How does a star "speak of the glory of God"? It's an inanimate object. It makes no sound, much less language — how does it speak?

By being a star.

How does a tree speak of the glory of God?

By being a tree.

How does a lion speak?

By roaring loud.

How does a flower speak?

By unfolding its color every spring.

When we see the world in the shape that God intended, the way it's supposed to be, God gets glory, *without a word.*

Think of my sunrise this morning. Some people look at a sunrise, and, sadly, all they see is beauty. No God, no wonder, no mystery, no hunger or thirst deep inside.

Other people look at a sunrise, and even if they have never *heard* the name Jesus, they see past the orange and yellow lasers in the sky to the beauty *behind* the beauty — and they awaken worship just by getting out of bed and looking out the window.

This is God's genius — the way he made the world.

As people made in God's image, we can join him in this ongoing creative work. As his partners, *we* can reshape the raw materials of his world in such a way that people see the beauty *behind* the beauty.

We can't make a sunrise — but we can make a painting or take a photograph.

We can't make a tree — but we can make a credenza.

We can't make the world — but we can *remake* it into a macchiato, a building, an app, a dress, a book, a meal, a school, a cure, a song, a business, or ten thousand other things in such a way that for those with eyes to see — the invisible God's *presence* and *beauty* are more than visible — they are glaring and inescapable.

This means we need to learn how to value beauty for beauty's sake. Maybe even for *God's* sake.

Remember that phrase from *Genesis*? "It was very good," that word "good" has to do with *aesthetic* good. It can be translated "lovely" or "beautiful." A tree can't be good or evil; it can only be beautiful or ugly. And God made it beautiful.

Nothing about creation says that God is a tightfisted, utilitarian, bean-counting pragmatist; God is a lavish, opulent, extravagant *artist*, and creation is his beauty on display.

In Genesis 2, we read, "The LORD God made all kinds of trees grow out of the ground — trees that were pleasing to the eye and good for food."[12] The rabbis wrestle with this verse because order is a big deal in Hebrew narrative. It's how you tell what really matters. And *first* we read that trees are

"pleasing to the eye"; *then* we read that they are "good for food."
This is telling.

Maybe this is why, historically, some of the world's greatest
artists have been followers of Jesus. They had such a compel-
ling vision of God that they *had* to reshape the world to help
others see who he is and what he's like. In fact, the first time
we read the phrase "filled with the Spirit of God," it's in the
book of *Exodus* ...

"See, I have chosen Bezalel son of Uri ... and I have filled
him with the Spirit of God, with wisdom, with understanding,
with knowledge and with all kinds of skills — *to make artistic
designs* for work in gold, silver and bronze, to cut and set
stones, to work in wood, and to engage in all kinds of crafts."[13]

So the first person who is "filled with the Spirit of God" isn't a
prophet or a priest or a king — he's an artist. And what was
the Spirit of God doing in him? Giving him "wisdom, with
understanding" and "knowledge" and "all kinds of skills" to
make art.

Theologian Ben Witherington III (how cool would that be, to
have *III* at the end of your name?) puts it this way:

"Sometimes Christians, especially frugal ones, think that the
creating of elaborate, beautiful works of art, worth lots of
money, is itself either a waste of money or at least not good

stewardship, if it is not simply sinful altogether. What this story suggests is just the opposite."[14]

Sometimes in our quest against injustice and greed and waste and in our passion to steward the wealth of the West in a kingdom-of-God-like way, it's easy to overreact and *devalue* the things that God himself values, like art or beauty. But that's a problem, because we worship an artist God.

As people made in his image — all work is artistic. All work is inherently creative. All work — from painting to parenting — is reshaping the raw materials of Planet Earth in such a way that it's how God intended, how it's supposed to be, all so humans can thrive as they see God's glory.

What I'm getting at is this: some people's work glorifies God *directly* — writing a book about God, preaching a sermon about God, singing a song about God, raising your children to love God, and so on. But most people's work glorifies God *indirectly* — and that's okay.

My point here isn't to "tone down all the Jesus talk" — no, Jesus should always be on the tip of our tongue. And glorifying God isn't the same thing as making disciples. Remember, we're called to do *both*. My point is that *what* you do can be done for God's *kavod*.

But it's not just *what* you do.

It's also *how* you do it.

Some of us don't have much control over what we do. We take a job, and then we do whatever the boss tells us to do. You would love to make something that's beautiful and sustainable and good for the earth and goes back into the local economy and does something about the plight of poverty or illiteracy or malaria in Nigeria — but these decisions are made a million miles above you on the corporate ladder. You sit in your cubicle or at your counter five days a week and do *exactly* what you're told. How do you glorify God?

In *how* you work.

We're the image of God, right? So our job is to mirror and mimic what God is like to the people around us. To show the world what God is like.

What does that look like? Well, here are a few ideas ...

God is hard working, so we should be hard working.

God is joyful and eager and proactive, so we should be cheerful and show up ten minutes early for our shift and volunteer when something difficult needs to be done.

God is honest and true, so we should be full of integrity — even when it means less money or no promotion.

Because we're made in the image of God. Here to make the invisible God visible. You're the priest of your office or classroom or home or job site. You're God's representative.

So much of this comes down to attitude. Think about how lousy on-the-job attitudes are. People gripe and whine and bad-mouth and gossip and slander and drag their feet like crazy. What if God's people were to cut across the grain and stick out like I do at my in-laws' house every Thanksgiving — the six-foot-two Swedish-looking guy in a house full of five-foot Cubans.

One of the leaders in our church works for a job-placement company. She sent me an email a while back telling me that whenever she can, she hires people from our church. Her boss — who is most definitely not a follower of Jesus — had just walked into her office and asked her to hire as many people as she can from "that church you go to" because they make the best employees around.

That's the dream, isn't it?

On one level, there's no difference between a barista who's a follower of Jesus and one who's not. They both make the exact same thing — really good coffee. But on another level, a barista who is a follower of Jesus should go about it with a love and humility and joy that is infectious and makes the people around them question why.

I think of that line in Paul's letter to the church in Thessalonica: "Make it your ambition to lead a quiet life: You should mind your own business and work with your hands, just as we told you, so that your daily life may win the respect of outsiders."[15]

So when we live well — when we work and rest — in a way that is quiet and hardworking and productive, and we don't grumble or mouth off or screw around or look at social media on work time — we "win the respect of outsiders."

Put another way, people see God's presence and beauty in how we live.

Put still *another* way, we glorify God.

There's another line in *2 Corinthians* where this idea of image is tied to God's glory. Paul writes, "We all, who with unveiled faces contemplate the Lord's glory, are being transformed into his image with ever-increasing glory, which comes from the Lord, who is the Spirit."[16]

So, as we "contemplate the Lord's glory" — as we stare deep into God's presence and beauty, call that worship, or call that getting up early to watch the sunrise — we are transformed into his image.

Wait a minute! I thought we already *were* the image of God? Yes, we are, but at this point in the book, we're still working through Genesis 1 and 2. We still have to talk about Genesis

3. I don't want to get ahead of myself, but to make a long story short, after the human rebellion, everything changed. We still bear God's image, but it's somehow been warped and twisted out of shape. It's still there, in every human on the planet, but for some people, it's beyond recognition. The good news is, as Jesus and the Spirit do their healing, saving work, we are transformed back into the image of the God who made us. And that image *is* glory in Paul's thinking. They are synonymous.

The more like Jesus we are, and the more like the image of God we are, the more people see of God's glory.

The early church father Irenaeus said, "The glory of God is a human being fully alive."[17]

In the same way that a tree glorifies God just by being a tree, we can glorify God just by being a really good human being.

And the world needs more really good human beings.

Now, to wrap up ...

Anybody like classical music?

I do, kind of. I feel the same way about classical music that I do about chess. I love it — in short, periodic spurts, but not all that often. I like the *idea* of classical music, just like I love the *idea* of chess — it makes me feel like I was born into a family from New York with money and educated at Yale. But sadly, I was born into a family without money in California and grew up on the Beatles, so it's a bit fake.

Anyway, back to classical music. There's a point coming, really.

One of my favorite composers is one of *everybody's* favorite composers — Johann Sebastian Bach. The guy was a prodigy. Over his lifetime he composed over a thousand songs.[18]

That we know of.

Did you know that he signed his music with two sets of initials — his own and then three more letters, *S.D.G.*? It's short for the Latin phrase *soli Deo gloria*, or "glory to God alone."

Here's the thing: most of Bach's music *didn't have any lyrics*. It was just really good music. But when you sit back and hear it — it does something to you. It's like you were sleeping through your entire life and you had no idea, but all of a sudden you wake up and you're *alive*. And that deep part of you — the God-craving part — comes to birth, and you start to sense that there's *more*. And whatever it is, or *he* is, you want in.

That's what *glory* does. One minute you're in the temple courtyard or at the symphony or walking past the credenza in your living room or sitting down to eat at your local food cart, and the next thing you know you're swimming in *kavod* . . .

Now, I'm well aware that most of us aren't Bach. Most of us aren't going to write a concerto or have our name on Wikipedia. But we all image God in our own small way.

What if our lives, every aspect of them — from what we do for work and rest to how we do it — were *soli Deo gloria*?

That would really be something.

Kazam! Machine

So we're starting to get a picture of what it means to be human. Hopefully it's coming into focus, getting clearer page by page. We're image bearers, created to *rule*, to partner with God in pushing and pulling the creation project forward, to *work* it, to draw out the earth's potential and unleash it for human flourishing — to cooperate with God in building a civilization where his people can thrive in his presence. And in this cosmic agenda, each of us has a *vocation*, a calling from God, a way that God wired us, somebody to be *and* something to do — because the two merge in perfect symmetry.

But if we're going to do all this to the *kavod* of God, that means we're going to have to get really good at whatever it is we do.

Really,

really,

really good.

If we're a teacher, we're going to have to teach our subject incredibly well.

If we're a software engineer, we're going to have to come up with something ingenious to make the world a better place.

If we're a full-time mom, we're going to have to unfold kids who know and follow Jesus, and as a result, live up to the breadth of their potential.

As my wife says all the time: we need to be the best version of ourselves.

But this isn't easy. In the day and age of smartphones and Wi-Fi and globalization and travel and nonstop multitasking — our culture is fractured and pulled in a thousand different directions.

We are fractured and pulled in a thousand different directions.

ADHD, stress, workaholism, burnout, connectivity — these are just words we come up with to name a world that is unraveling at the seams.

There's a saying I *hate*; maybe you've heard it:

"Jack of all trades, master of none."

This is what every guy says when he fixes something around the house, Oh, you know me, I'm a Jack of all trades, master of none. Ha-ha.

Honestly, I don't think it's funny. It's too close to home. Far too many of us don't really have one thing that we're *good* at.

Did you know that saying is actually a misquote? The original saying goes back to Mr. hundred-dollar-bill himself — Benjamin Franklin.[1] What he actually said was that every person should be a "Jack of all trades, master of *one*." He was making the exact opposite point. He was saying that every one of us should get incredibly good at one thing. Sure, be well-rounded, know a little about everything, dabble if you want, fine. As long as you're a master/craftsman/specialist/expert/scholar/author-ity/black belt/maestro of *one*.

I think he was on to something.

Now, your one thing might be really narrow like cabinetry or early childhood education or Egyptology (yes, that's a thing) or teaching the Bible or how to make falafel.

Or your one thing might be really broad, like sales or manage-ment or customer service. Either way is fine.

But there's something about a man or a woman who is really good at what they do.

When I watch my wife, Tammy, with our three kids — she's incredible ...

When I watch my buddy Ryan, a graphic designer, develop a new brand ...

When I watch my coworker Gerald, a pastor at our church, lead people ...

The other day I was in San Francisco. Every time I'm there I hit up this men's clothing shop where they do custom shirts at a great price. My body is *weird*. I honestly don't fit into anything off-the-rack, at least not well. My torso is a medium, my arms are an XXL, and my neck is an XS, dinky. Plus, my shoulders are crooked and one arm is longer than the other. To quote one tailor, "Your body is jacked up." Thank you? So when I discovered this menswear shop, it was like striking gold. Last time I was there, I ordered a new shirt. It takes a little while to pick out materials and for the guy to take your measurements, so you end up in a conversation. The tailor, this guy Ryan, was fascinating.[2] He had moved out from Nashville to do "suiting." I didn't even know that was a profession. His *passion* is suits. He thinks men waste money and time and materials buying a dozen cheap, low-quality suits over a lifetime when really they just need one or two quality, well-made, custom-fit suits. So right now he works out of this shop, but his dream is to do suiting full-time.

Whenever I meet somebody like that, something about them, at a subliminal level, says, This is what a person made in the image of God looks like. And for those with eyes to see, I think it glorifies God.

This is what we see in Jesus of Nazareth. Most of us don't think about Jesus in this way, as a worker who was really good at his job. But he was. He had a trade.

Remember that before he was a well-known rabbi, he was a *tekton* working in obscurity for *three decades*. Working hard six days a week, and then resting on the Sabbath, as an act of worship, and then doing it all over again.

If Jesus came today he could have been a software engineer or a high school drama teacher or a graphic-novel writer or a diesel mechanic or a journalist for the *New York Times*. In other words, *he could very well do what you do*. He could live in your house or apartment, work your job, have your education and skill set, and *none* of that would keep him from a 24/7 life in the kingdom of God.[3]

In fact, discipleship to Jesus is about one simple question: if Jesus were me, if he lived in my city, had my job, my education, made my salary, had my family, *how would he live?*

That is *the* question.

For Jesus' followers, life is nothing more than the search for a good answer.

Discipleship is about learning how to become a good human being. And how to live into *both* your callings, to make disciples *and* to create culture.

At my church we have newly married groups because we really believe that marriage matters, and that if we're going to follow Jesus, we need to be good spouses.

But why don't we have "newly hired accountant" groups and "newly hired investment banker" groups and "newly hired fireman (or firewoman)" groups? After all, if we really believe that what we do *matters*, and if we're going to follow Jesus, then we need to be good accountants and investment bankers and firefighters.

Do you see your work as an essential part of your discipleship to Jesus and as the primary way that you join him in his work of renewal?

If not, you should.

Learning how to become a really good mom or dad to your children and a really good disciple of Jesus *are the exact same thing.*

Learning how to become a really good screenwriter in Hollywood and a really good disciple of Jesus *are the exact same thing*.

Learning how to become a really good employee for a landscape maintenance company and a really good disciple of Jesus *are the exact same thing*.

Are you getting my drift?

Yes, Jesus was the template for what Godness looks like. If you want to know what God is like, look at Jesus of Nazareth. But the mystery of the incarnation is that he was *also* the template for what real, true *humanness* looks like. He's the Son of God *and* he's the "son of Adam." If you want to know what a human being, fully awake and alive, ruling over the world as a conduit for the Creator God's love looks like in flesh and blood — then look at Jesus.

Let's take a few minutes to think through his life and work because I think it could reframe how we think about *our* life and work . . .

One of the first stories we read about Jesus in the Gospels is his baptism. It's this defining, revelatory movement where he goes under the waters in the Jordan and then comes back out in John the Baptizer's arms, and then heaven itself is rent open and the audible voice of God says, "You are my Son, whom I love; with you I am well pleased."[4]

Now, "son of God" wasn't just a way of saying that Jesus had a special relationship with the Father, although there's no doubt that's true. But in the Hebrew Scriptures, "son of God" was a name for Israel, and then later for the Messiah, Israel's representative, a kinglike figure on the horizon who would draw Israel's story to its climax and usher in the kingdom of God.[5]

So Jesus' baptism is the turning point in his life, where he gets incredible clarity about who he is and what he's called to do. No doubt he had an idea for years, growing up in Nazareth, but this is *the* moment — inaugurating his life's work.

And Jesus, newly armed with a vocation, with a calling from God, goes out "proclaiming the good news of God. 'The time has come,' he said, 'The kingdom of God has come near.' "[6]

Within days word is out on the street there's a rabbi named Jesus who is preaching radical, evocative, dangerous, exciting new things, as well as healing the sick, casting out demons, standing up to the religious elite, and, some people even say, raising the dead. In fact, some people think he's *more* than a rabbi, he's a prophet, or even more, the Messiah. And some people think he could be even *more* than that . . .

On his second day of work, Jesus goes out early for prayer. His disciples find him a few hours later and say, "Everybody is looking for you." *Vanity Fair* is calling; they want to do a piece.

Anderson Cooper is waiting outside. The *Times* shot an email about an op-ed.

You're expecting Jesus to say, Let's do it. But instead, he says, "Let us go somewhere *else* — to the nearby villages — so I can preach there also. That is why I have come."[7]

That's Jesus for *no*.

Why would Jesus turn down such an incredible opportunity? *Because he knew what he was called to do.* Which means he also knew what he *wasn't* called to do. He wasn't just called to Capernaum. He was called to Galilee as a region, and then later to Israel itself. And "so he traveled throughout Galilee, preaching in their synagogues and driving out demons."[8] And as he goes all over the north of Israel, doing his thing, the writer Mark has this word he uses over and over for people's response to Jesus' work — *ekplesso.* It's translated "amazed" or "marveled" or "overwhelmed."[9] People are blown away by Jesus' skill. As one observer put it, "He has done everything well."[10]

About three years into his work, Jesus "set his face to go to Jerusalem."[11] The imagery here is of when you clench your jaw and drive forward, not looking to the right or left. He's dead set on the capital city and, behind that, his death and resurrection. This is the apex of his "career." And when he finally gets there, after three *years* of buildup, he prays this thought-provoking prayer to his Father:

"I have brought you glory on earth by finishing the work you gave me to do."**12**

In one version of Jesus' story, his last words are, "It is *finished*."**13**

How could Jesus say that? There was *so much* work left to be done! The world was still in shambles. A black hole of need. His disciples were in hiding. The church in Jerusalem was 120 people on a good day. The New Testament wasn't even written yet. The religious elite were hostile toward him. He was an enemy of the state. Injustice was ubiquitous. And he says, That's a wrap.

There is *a lot* we can learn from Jesus about work.

Shocking, I know.

A few observations. First, Jesus worked with a staggering amount of focus.

The need for this is greater now than it's ever been. We live in what one thinker calls the "iWorld"**14** — the day of iPhones and social media and internet at your fingertips and ten-lane freeways and VISA and FedEx and this nasty demon called the microwave. And so we always feel pulled in a million directions. And we end up stressed out, tired, falling behind, uptight, raw, on meds, and addicted to caffeine.

We're trying to do too much.

To focus, we need to know what we're called by God to do, *and* what we're not called to do.

Who we *are,*

and who we *aren't.*

I love that story in John's gospel where John the Baptizer, who was also really good at his job, was fielding questions from skeptical religious leaders in Jerusalem. Clearly God's hand was on this young prophet, but nobody could figure out what category to put him in.

"Who are you? Are you Elijah?"

"I am not."

"Are you the Prophet?" (Another name for the Messiah)

"No."

Finally they said, *"Who are you?* Give us an answer ..."

And he started to quote another prophet, Isaiah: *"I am the voice of one calling in the wilderness,* 'Make straight the way for the Lord.' "[15]

Notice that he starts by saying who he's *not*. It's just as important to know who you're *not* and what you aren't called to, as it is to know who you are and what you *are* called to. Because the clearer your sense of identity and calling are, the more you can focus on what God made you to do.

You start by saying *yes* to God's calling on your life, and then you say *no* to everything else.

Here's my takeaway: be yourself. The real, true you. The one God himself created. Don't try to be somebody else.

We all come into this world with an end in mind, a destiny, a *calling*. But so often that calling is hijacked by our fear or insecurity. Or it's beat to a pulp by our upbringing or abusive father or a mean friend in middle school. Or it's dead on arrival because the economy's in the tank. Or it's pushed off to the side by our jealousy, wishing we were somebody else.

Most of us spend years of our short, ephemeral life trying to be somebody we're not. Trying to be like our mentor or our hero or some ideal we aspire to or some person our parents want us to be, or our generation wants us to be, or what our friends think is cool — and we spin our wheels and spiral out of control until we end up nowhere but the end of our rope.

There's an ancient rabbinic saying that's worth quoting here. The legendary Rabbi Zusya, when he was an old man, said this: "In the coming world, they will not ask me: 'Why were you not Moses?' They will ask me: 'Why were you not Zusya?' "[16]

Our job isn't to fit into some mold or prove something to the world; it's to unlock who God's made us to be, and then go be it.

Usually God's calling is a short list — just a few things. In my case, I'm called to lead my church, teach the Scriptures, and bring my family along for the ride. That's what I'm saying *yes* to, which means, I have to say *no* all the time.

I'm a pastor, and so my job comes freighted with a lot of expectations. People want me to lead the church, give vision, have something TED-talk quality to chat about for forty min-utes *every* Sunday, meet with fifty people every week for cof-fee, keep the staff healthy, mentor three hundred people, read the Bible in Greek and Hebrew every morning, go through a thousand books a year, pop on social media a few times a day, write a blog, pump out a book every so often, have the picture-perfect marriage and family, be really involved in justice in my neighborhood — oh, and stay "healthy."

Now, that's all great stuff. Superpastor would kill it at that job. But I'm not superpastor. I'm John Mark. Obviously I can't do all that in one lifetime.

So I'm constantly saying *no*.

"John Mark, you should mentor this new graduate."

"No."

"Why not?"

"I already mentor three guys, and that's all I have time for."

"But he's amazing!"

"Sorry."

"John Mark, you should start this new ministry."

"That's a great idea, but it's not 'the work the Father gave me to do.'"

"Hey, so-and-so's in town and they want to hang out tonight — they could get you more Twitter followers."

"I would *love* to, but I'm called to father my three kids, and tonight we're building a fort in the living room."

To borrow from the language of Jesus, you gotta figure what the "work the Father gave you to do" is.

And then you need to learn the art of saying no. To *good things*. A smart man once said, "Good is the enemy of best."[17]

Some of us end up doing a lot of *good* things, but we never get around to doing the *best* thing. Because when you get sucked into the tyranny of the urgent (what a great phrase, by the way), you put off what's really important. When you say *yes* to *everything*, you say *yes* to *nothing*. The work the Father gave you to do gets put on the back burner, at the bottom of the to-do pile. This is a tragedy because you're robbing the world of your much-needed contribution.

Can I just give you permission to say *no*?

Do I have that authority?

I guess not, but what the heck, I give it anyways. This coming week, you have the freedom to say *no*. I commission you. When you get that amazing opportunity that you don't really have time for — say *no*. When you plan out your week — say *no*. When you sit down in January to map out the coming year — *say no*. And say *no* to good things. You gotta be ruthless. Not because you're a selfish jerk and you don't care about anybody, but because you know who you are and you *have* to do the Father's work.

So, that's the first takeaway for me from Jesus' life. An unnerving level of focus. The other observation I see is the high quality of Jesus' work. It wasn't haphazard or sloppy. It was really well-done.

I love that line, "He has done everything well." When you figure out what it is you're called to, and say *no* to everything else, it frees you up to do that one thing *well* — this, in turn, is what opens up doors to do *more* of whatever it is you do so well.

There's a line in the Hebrew wisdom literature that I love ...

"Do you see someone skilled in their work? They will serve before kings; they will not serve before officials of low rank."[18]

When you're good at what you do, you end up in front of kings.

It shouldn't surprise us that Jesus' work was superlative. After all, he's the embodiment of the Creator God. Look around you; creation is incredible. God doesn't do cheap, low-grade, half-baked work. He's not lazy. He doesn't make junk. He has a value for excellence and artistry and quality of materials and design. And it's not because he is a perfectionist. Although, I guess he is perfection ... It's because he is *love*. All of creation's excellence is an act of generous, creative, self-giving love for the world.

A genuine, authentic love of excellence isn't rooted in greed or narcissism or materialism — that's dualism talking. It's rooted in *love*, for God and others. A desire to serve God and his world well.

Have you ever been to a European cathedral? One of the really good ones? Notre Dame in Paris? Westminster Abbey in London? Some of them took *generations* to build. And if you look at them closely, you notice that every nook and cranny is covered in rich, ornate detailing. Even the ceiling. Even the parts of the cathedral that *nobody can see*. Why? If you were a craftsman a thousand years ago, why would you put all that effort and energy into something nobody would even see?

Maybe because God would see it.

Maybe he would even *value* it.

Dorothy Sayers, this spunky, rebellious British writer from half a century ago, said that the best way to serve others with our work is to "serve the work." What she meant was that the best way to love and serve others with our job was just to be really good at our jobs. If you're a pilot, the best way to serve your passengers is to be a really good pilot. If you're a chef, the best way to serve your customers is to make really good food. If you're a neurosurgeon, the best way to serve your patients is to be a really good doctor.

Sayers went on to say, "The church's approach to an intelligent carpenter is usually confined to exhorting him to not be drunk and disorderly in his leisure hours and to come to church on Sundays. What the church should be telling him is this: that the very first demand that his religion makes upon him is that he should make good tables."[19]

That is money.

Now, this doesn't mean you have to be the best. In the day and age of globalization, competition is fierce, cruel, and merciless. And thanks to social media none of us feel anywhere close to as cool as everybody else. The fact is there will always be somebody smarter than you, more gifted than you, and just flat out *better* than you.

Sorry, I know that's not very inspiring, but you know I'm right.

The writer Paul put it this way: "We have different gifts, according to the grace given to each of us."[20]

So we all have gifts, but we don't all have the same dosage of grace. Some of us have more; others have less.

And that's okay.

Your job isn't to be the best in your field, just the best version of *yourself.*

My teaching mentor is this guy Mike.[21] He took me under his wing when I was about twenty-five and I've learned a ton from him. Brilliant dude. He could talk about ant-hive social dynamics for forty minutes and you would be on the edge of your seat. He's smart, well-read, edgy, and *funny.*

I will never be as good of a teacher as Mike. I work twice as long on my teachings, and they are about half as good. And that's just fine. Because I'm not called to be as good as or better than Mike. I'm just supposed to do a good job at being myself. To take my background, experience, education, brains, skill, or lack of skill, go to work every day, and do the best I can.

But that said, if we're going to get really good at something, it's going to take time. And effort. And energy. Lots of it.

The graphic designer Frank Chimero tells a story about this chef from a prestigious restaurant in New York City called Momofuku. One day he saw his sous-chef cutting a corner and came down hard on him, "We don't work like that here. We do things the long, hard, stupid way."[22]

The long, hard, stupid way.

So incredibly good.

But working the long, hard, stupid way takes a *lot* of time. And getting good at what you do takes even longer. Years. No, *decades*. A lifetime of learning and training and education and practice and self-discipline and not giving up on the pursuit of excellence as an act of *abad*, service and worship.

One of my best friends is named Robbie. He's a designer for Adidas. We live in the same neighborhood with about a dozen other people and do life together around the gospel,[23] so I get to watch him close up. Robbie is one of the top designers for his company. If you've ever worn a pair of Adidas shoes, there's a really good chance Robbie either made them or was involved. And Robbie *loves* his job. He's like a little kid at play.

The other day he showed me his fifth grade report card, Mrs. McAvoy's class. His grades were fine, but at the bottom was a note from the teacher:

"Less athletic shoe drawing might prove beneficial."

True story! He framed it for over his desk — which is the adult equivalent of I'll *show* you! I love that story, probably because it taps into my innate desire to show my grade school teachers how much better I am than they said I would be. But as funny as Robbie's report card is, it shows he's been honing his skill *since fifth grade*.

Is it any wonder that now in his thirties he's at the top of his field? He's serving in front of kings . . .

In the early '90s, a study was done by a German psychologist for the elitist Academy of Music in Berlin. He found the best musicians were *not* those with the most raw, innate talent; they were those who practiced way, *way* more than all the other students. He put the number for mastery of an instrument at ten thousand hours. Since then, his study has been redone dozens of times in every field imaginable, and it's always the same number — ten thousand hours. That's how long it takes to get really good at something. If you practice your tail off, that should take you about a *decade.*[24]

Are you willing to work that hard? For that long?

One of my favorite designers is a guy named Charlie Eames. He trained as an architect and then started to design furniture right out of school. After a frustrating interruption called World War 2, he went back to furniture. His dream was to take plywood — this cheap, easy-to-come-by, sturdy material he worked with during the war — and figure out how to bend it to make chairs. His end goal was affordable but well-made modern design for the postwar masses. That's what he said *yes* to. But it took him years. Years teetering on the edge of bankruptcy. Years working part-time as a Hollywood set painter to pay the bills. Years of failure. Years of slugging it out.

At one point he was living in Pasadena with his wife, Ray. They had moved out from the Midwest to give the molded-plywood dream yet another try. They rented a cheap apartment, and he worked on his invention — a machine to bend wood. They called it the Kazam! Machine. They weren't allowed to do work like that in the apartment, so he sneaked all the materials in at night. At one point he needed more power, and so he strung a heavy cord out the window, climbed up the telephone pole, and plugged right into the transformer. And he built the Kazam! Machine in his living room, out of 2x4 scraps and a bicycle pump. I swear I'm not making this up. In the end, he finally got it to work, and, well, his Eames LCW chair from 1946 won the award for the best design of the twentieth century.[25]

I have one in my living room. I gotta tell you, it's really something.

So, after all that, here's what I'm saying:

Do one thing.

And do one thing *well*.

And do that one thing well as an act of service and love for the world and to the glory of God.

That last part is the key. The cultural milieu we live in is one of celebrityism. The temptation, when you get really good at something, is to do it to serve and love *yourself*, not the world, and to do it for your *own* glory, not God's. It's so easy for gifted people to fall into pride, hubris, shameless self-promoting, and self-aggrandizement. It's lame.

If you're really good at whatever it is you do, you don't need to tell the rest of us. We'll know. Beautiful things don't ask for attention.

God is looking for people he can give more "grace" to. People who can *handle* grace, with grace.

After all, God is looking for people he can rule the world with. And you just might be one.

What if God's people were known as the best carpenters and the best CEOs and the most educated teachers and the most creative artists and the most ingenious writers *and* as the most humble, self-effacing, down-to-earth, servant-hearted, loving people around? I think that would make God very happy.

To end, my brother-in-law Steve, the designer, just did an interview with J. Crew. One of the questions was, Do you have a design philosophy that sets the tone for your work? This was his answer:

"Good design is putting our best forward; it is working hard to bring beauty into the world. When I see something that is brilliant it wrecks me in the best sort of way. I am also constantly returning to this idea that we were created with the ability to create and that makes our God the most generous of all. I'm humbled after I complete every new project, and as I stand there with a big silly grin on my face, I feel his presence and approval."

Yeah, I got nothing to add to *that*.

Cursed is the ground

Okay, now it's time to deal with the elephant in the room.

All this talk about work is just a tad unrealistic. (Okay, there I go again. It's *very* unrealistic.) I mean, a theology of work that's rooted in the Garden of Eden is ignoring the obvious — we don't live in Eden anymore.

My address isn't 197 SW Euphrates Road.

My wife's name isn't Eve.

And I don't commute in the nude to my job as a gardener and animal-namer: I call this one *possum*!

The world I call home is anything but a garden.

God's original vision of Adam and Eve as kings and queens,

ruling *under* his generous, loving authority and *over* the earth, drawing out the world's potential and repurposing it for God's *kavod* and human flourishing — oh man, it was beautiful.

And short lived.

Sadly, Genesis 2 is followed by Genesis 3 . . .

"Now the serpent was more crafty than any of the wild animals the LORD God had made. He said to the woman, 'Did God really say, "You must not eat from any tree in the garden"?' "

This is why a lot of people don't trust the Bible. A talking snake? Really?

If that's you, suspend judgment for a few minutes. Remember this story is *thousands* of years old. It was probably around for a millennium as an oral tradition before it was ever written down.

Is it poetry? Narrative? A metaphor? *Literal?*

You're missing the point. What should jump off the page to you is the serpent — this embodiment of evil — was an *animal.*

Remember, Adam and Eve were called to "rule" over "every living creature that moves on the ground."[1] But instead, in a catastrophic inversion of the created order, an animal — *that Adam himself named!* — ruled over *them.*

This is the exact *opposite* of what was supposed to happen.

Adam was supposed to "take care" of the Garden — to guard it and watch over it — but instead he let evil incarnate right into the center of Eden, and he abused its most precious resource — the tree of the knowledge of good and evil.

He was the first king of the world, and tragically, he was a colossal failure.

And the fallout is disastrous. God comes to Eden in search of his king and queen. Where are they? Hiding in the bushes. So the very place that was once "delight"[2] — a place of safety and vulnerability and beauty — is now a place of fear and shame and regret. And the Creator, who so far has been marked by creativity and power and generosity and freedom and love, does something odd and out of character — he *curses* his image.

And Adam and Eve are cursed differently.

God says to the woman, "I will make your pains in childbearing very severe; with painful labor you will give birth to children."[3]

So Eve is cursed in childbirth. What was originally a good pain — a healthy sense of creative energy — is now "very severe." I've watched Tammy give birth to two children, and trust me, this language is more than fitting.

Then God says to Adam, "Cursed is the ground because of you; through painful toil you will eat food from it all the days of your life. It will produce thorns and thistles for you, and you will eat the plants of the field. By the sweat of your brow you will eat your food until you return to the ground, since from it you were taken; for dust you are and to dust you will return."[4]

The man is cursed in his relationship to the ground. What was once life-giving, is now exhausting, hard, and difficult. There are "thorns and thistles" — sharp pain — in everything we put our hand to.

Both the family and the field are cursed by the Creator himself.

Now, make sure you pay close attention to the language. A lot of people misread it and think that work is the curse. Nothing could be further from the truth. Remember what we said early on? Work is the *blessing*. "God *blessed* them and said . . . *rule* . . ."

Work isn't the curse any more than children are.

(Parents, no snide comments here.)

Work *is* cursed. And so is childbearing.

That's different.

Curse here doesn't mean a voodoo spell. It means that in the wake of humans' sin, there are far-reaching, irreversible, toxic changes to the experience of family and field.

What was once all joy is now a mixed bag. There's still a lot of joy, for sure, but there's also a lot of frustration.

Both childbearing and gardening are now called "painful labor." And the language of "thorns and thistles" is symbolic for all culture making. *All* human effort for civilization is now cursed with a nagging sense of dissatisfaction.

Fatigue, burnout, back pain, ibuprofen, strife, litigation, greed, waste, poverty, injustice, wishing you had more vacation time — *all* this comes in the wake of Eve's first bite.

You might not be able to generate an income from what you love to do, or maybe even from what you're called to do, and so you'll have to either give it up or get a "day job" and do it in your free time.

Or you might be in a job you love, but the people you work with are annoying, and the gossip and elbow-throwing and cutthroat economy is a weight on your soul.

And it's only in the First World that we can even *think* this way.

In the developing world — also known as the *majority world* because *most* of the seven-plus billion people on earth live there — people live hand-to-mouth. Working all day in a small field just to eke out enough food to survive. Those with ambition move to the city where they usually end up in a factory on an assembly line. Nothing could be more dehumanizing. The worker is disconnected from the product. So there's no sense of pride or accomplishment after a long day's work. You're basically a living cog in a machine, stuck in a hot, humid, dark room, watching the clock on the wall, tick-tock, tick-tock, day, after day, after day.

Even in the so-called First World, a lot of people end up working for a multinational corporation. They have no sense of connection to the product they make or the community they serve, no voice or influence or seat at the table — just an ugly, utilitarian cubicle with a florescent light overhead and a job that feels insignificant.

Plus, you have the quickly evaporating middle class here in the U.S. One journalist recently said we're moving toward a dystopian future with a "digital world feudalism," as a technology-savvy, educated minority rule over the masses of minimum-wage, service-sector employees.[5]

All over the world the workplace is marked by a sense of "this isn't how it's supposed to be" — unjust labor ethics, gender discrimination, child labor, human trafficking, the ever-widening gap between rich and poor ...

It comes as no surprise that 70 percent of Americans are "not engaged" or "actively disengaged" with their work.[6]

Seventy percent. A huge number of people wake up in the morning and think, *I gotta do something else,* or *Three more days until the weekend.*

This is because we were created to rule *on behalf* of God, as his kings and queens, in partnership with the Creator, but instead we now rule for ourselves, looking out for number one, no matter the expense to the earth or its inhabitants.

And so the *selem,* the image, who was supposed to take the Garden and spread it out all over the world is instead in exile from the Garden and driving the world into the ground.

We can just barely see Eden through our rearview mirror …

Yet still, in spite of all this, so many of us look to our work — whatever it is we *do* — for our identity and even significance. And this isn't all bad. Who we are and what we do are inseparable, as I said before. But when we *define* who we are by what we do and we're stuck in a job or life we don't like, we're on dangerous ground.

One of the first stories we read after the Eden debacle is about a building project in a city called Babel.[7]

We read, "As people moved eastward, they found a plain in Shinar." This is good. Human starts to spread out over the earth. Adam's sons and daughters were called to "fill the earth." The story is heading in the right direction.

But then it all goes south.

"They said to each other, 'Come, let's make bricks and bake them thoroughly.' They used brick instead of stone, and tar for mortar."

Fascinating. They come up with a brand-new technology — the brick. A giant leap forward in civilization. Now they can build cheaper, faster, and *taller*.

"Come, let us build ourselves a city, with a tower that reaches to the heavens, so that we may make a name for ourselves; otherwise we will be scattered over the face of the whole earth."

Wait a minute. "Scattered over the face of the whole earth" is a *good* thing. It's what they were *supposed* to do. But in an act of rebellion, they say, No, we're staying right here, and we're building a city, with a tower that reaches to the heavens.

This is interesting. The heavens are where God is. So they are looking to this building project — to work — for a pseudo-spirituality, a sense of meaning and purpose that can only be found in God himself.

And all this is "so that we may make a name for ourselves." They're looking to work for identity and status. As a rating system to see how they measure up to the people around them.

Your tower is only how high? Oh, I'm so sorry ...

Of course, the story is a disaster. Hubris always leads to strife and in-fighting and eventually implosion. In the end, "The LORD scattered them from there over all the earth, and they stopped building the city."

But after who-knows-how-many millennia of so-called evolution, are we any different? Any better?

Every year or two the record is broken on the tallest building in the world. Right now it's the Burj Khalifa in Dubai, jutting 2,722 feet into the atmosphere, but by the time you're reading this book, I'm sure it will be another building, in another city.[8]

My point is that as human beings, we have this slant to look to our work for significance we can only find in God.

When we uncouple our work from God, work becomes a sort of god in and of itself.

It's called workaholism. Work can be just as addictive as any narcotic. Even if it's hard and difficult and frustrating at times, that sense of accomplishment and accumulation, that sense of another foot higher on your own personal tower of Babel — is a buzz a lot of us crave.

Technology has made it easier than ever to become a work addict. We don't have to get in the car or on the subway and go to work anymore; we just have to grab our phone or pop open our laptop and the office comes to us. It's like slipping a needle into a vein on your arm — you know it's dangerous, but it feels *so good*.

But workaholism is more than an addiction; it's a twisted kind of worship, a search for meaning and purpose in what we *do*.

That's the insidious and self-deceiving thing about work — it can be too much of a good thing. Maybe what you do is good, even great, it's for human flourishing, it's vital to the world, but *why* you're doing it is all off.

Nowhere is this more true than in my job. I gave up the idea of ever having a pure motive a long time ago. It's *so easy* for me to do the right thing — teach the Scriptures, write a book about God, lead the church into a new venture, do justice, whatever — for all the wrong reasons. For myself, for money, for people to think I'm amazing — anything my cracked heart can conjure up. My guess is I'm not the only one with the occasional dubious motivation behind my work.

One person works hard as an act of worship to God and an expression of love and service to the world.

Another person works hard because they are subconsciously thinking, *If I can just close this deal* or *make this sale* or *get this promotion* or *make it as a novelist* or *get recognition as a _____*, then *I'll be happy.*

It's Babel all over again. The human quest to "build a tower to the heavens," to search for identity and significance in our work.

Maybe this isn't you at all. Maybe you're thinking, What's *wrong* with these people? I *hate* my job. Maybe for you, it's not work that's your tower of Babel, it's rest.

"Live for the weekend" is your motto. Remember what we said earlier, for *so many* people work is a *means to an end*. It's something we do, so we can go do something *else*. The goal is to make as much money as possible, with as little effort and energy as possible, so that we can get off work and go play. Go do whatever it is we love.

And just like work, a lot of people look to rest or play or leisure for a sense of identity.

"I'm a musician."

"I'm an athlete."

"I'm a backpacker."

"I'm a surfer."

"I'm a reader."

"I'm a fashion blogger."

We're starving for a sense of identity, and even more, for belonging in a community. This desire isn't bad, at all. It's latent in all of us from birth because it was put there by *God*. But when we search for identity and belonging in what we do for fun, instead of in God and his people, we turn music or sport or fashion or fishing or whatever it is we love into a little-*g* god, and we come up empty every time.

Now, whether your god of choice is work or rest or some amalgamation of the two, *both* are on a collision course with disillusionment.

Work, because no matter how great your job is, it's never *enough*. Every time you cut down a weed in the garden, three more take its place. Work is a to-do list that never ends. We constantly feel like we're behind. This is exhausting as the years of our life tick down.

And rest, because whatever it is — that vacation, your trip to Italy, the weekend seeing your favorite band live, surfing the North Shore — it will never be *quite* perfect. So in the end you feel the void. We're hardwired to *contribute* to the world, but when all we do is *consume*, no matter how great it is, after a while we feel empty.

We have this nagging sense of, *What's it all for?*

There's an entire book in the Bible written about this. It's called *Ecclesiastes*, and it was written, ironically, by a king. A *ruler.* A guy who started out really good — as a potential replacement for Adam himself — but ended really, really bad. He started to hunt for satisfaction everywhere but in God himself. *Ecclesiastes* is basically his rant on how "everything is meaningless" and he can't find what he's searching for "under the sun" (a euphemism for this life apart from God).

He tries *everything*. Education, laughter, fun, pleasure, hedonism, success, wealth — *everything*. Including work.

Listen to him go off ...

"I hated life, because the work that is done under the sun was grievous to me. All of it is meaningless, a chasing after the wind.... So my heart began to despair over all my toilsome labor under the sun. For a person may labor with wisdom, knowledge and skill, and then they must leave all they own to another who has not toiled for it. This too is meaningless and a great misfortune. What do people get for all the toil and anxious striving with which they labor under the sun? All their days their work is grief and pain; even at night their minds do not rest. This too is meaningless."[9]

Now, before you get all depressed and cry, keep in mind that this is a picture of work "under the sun." This is what work looks like if we do it apart from God. Hopefully, our entire outlook on work is drastically different. But still, we can all relate to the king's angst at some level.

Eventually, most of our work will be washed away by history. The book you are reading right now might sell well for a few years. Who knows, there's an off chance it might even make it onto a bestseller list (okay, probably not). But even if that were to happen, in a century or two *nobody* will remember it, and in another century or two it will literally turn to dust.

If I'm in it for myself, and if this life is all there is, then the king is right. This is all meaningless. Thankfully, I'm *not* just in it for myself (just partially for myself, *ouch*), and this life is *not* all there is. Resurrection is on the horizon. But still, in spite of that, at times it does feel a bit meaningless. Or at least, like a bit of a letdown.

This is especially true for my generation. I'm a millennial, what the *Huffington Post* called the "GYPSY"[10] generation.

(Please, don't make any jokes. We know we're screwed up, okay?)

Our grandparents' generation grew up during the Great Depression, and then lived through World War 2. They were just happy to have a job. Safety and security was a high enough goal to shoot for. If they could pay the mortgage and put food on the table, they were happy.

Our parents' generation took it one step further. They wanted more than a steady job that could pay the bills. They wanted to make money. A lot of it. Buy stuff. Play. Go on vacation somewhere tropical.

But my generation left the atmosphere. We aren't happy with just a high-paying job, a nice car, and the occasional expensive vacation. We want our dreams to come true. We want *fulfillment* from our work.

And we have a shot at it. We're the children of affluence. A lot of the jokes about how millennials live at home until thirty and goof off and are flaky and immature and travel a lot make it sound like this is something new.

Honestly, this is how rich kids have always behaved.[11]

Oh, we don't think of ourselves as wealthy. I was born in a classic middle-class family in a California suburb, but in reality, I grew up a child of privilege. I was, and still am, rich.

And wealth means we have options. More than any other generation before us. This is good *and* bad, depending on how you see it.

For *thousands* of years you did what your father or mother before you did.

If your father was a king, you were a king. If he was a farmer, you were a farmer, usually on the same plot of land. If he was a Sherpa, he raised you to be an even better Sherpa.

One of my friend's last name is Buckstaber. It's German for "bookmaker." His great-great-great grandfather was a book-maker. And his father before him. *And his father before him.*

If your last name is Smith, the odds are your great-great-great grandfather was a blacksmith.

My point is that most people down through history and around the world today don't get to choose what they do for a liv-ing. That's a luxury of the rich. My church does a lot of work in Zimbabwe, which used to be an economic powerhouse — it was called the "bread basket of Africa" — until a despotic *ruler* named Mugabe came to power. He's essentially wrecked the country. Inflation is at 89,700,000,000,000,000,000,000 percent. I don't even know how to *say* that number. And unemployment is at *85 percent.*[12] Nine out of ten people in Zimbabwe don't even *have* a job. They don't wake up and think, *What's my dream?* They think, *How can I survive?* They will do *anything* just to scrape out a living.

But here in the West, we have the exact opposite problem. We have *so many* options that it's intimidating. I could be a pastor, a writer, an architect, a designer, a restaurant owner, a journal-ist — any number of things. And I'm thankful for all the options. But the array of choices can be *paralyzing.*

What if we miss it?

And once we finally settle on a career, our expectations are so, so high. Food on the table might have been enough for grandma, or a nice TV to watch the game for dad, but not for us. We want to do something we *love*.

Once again, *I'm all for this.* One of the reasons I'm writing this book is to give you a swift kick in the pants to go chase after your dreams. Yes, this is a luxury of the rich — so take advantage of it!

But even if we are successful, here's a few things to note . . .

(Heads up, this next part isn't exactly a pep talk.)

First, our dreams will probably take *way* longer than we're expecting. Years, if not *decades* of straight-up hard work. Remember that ten-thousand-hours thing? There will be days, even *months*, where you roll over in the morning and think, *Another day . . .* There's a reason patience is fast becoming a thing of the past. It's brutally hard.

Second, other people will do a lot better than us. No matter how smart or hard working or gifted or charismatic we are, *there will always be somebody better than us.*

And thanks to social media, we now have a new way to torment each other. Image crafting makes us look way more successful than we actually are. We curate the best parts of our lives, and hide everything else under the rug. So as we go out into the world, we see people, and from a distance, it looks like they are wildly successful, when in reality, they are slugging it out just like we are. But we don't see reality. We see an Instagram post. And to make matters worse, in a culture of celebrityism, we tell the stories of the dinky minority that *are* widely successful at a young age. Making us feel all the more inferior.

Third — and stay with me, the depressing part is almost over, I promise — if and when we finally "make it" and are success-ful, it's never quite as great as we hoped. Or if it is, then the euphoric feeling of a dream come true is ephemeral. It doesn't last very long.

So most of us live with a profound sense of letdown and disillusionment.

A pair of sociologists used this formula:

"Happiness equals reality minus expectations."[13]

That's a scientific way of saying that we all have expectations. If you do *better* than your expectations, then the odds are you will be happy. But if your life doesn't measure up to what you were hoping for, then the odds are, no matter how successful you are, you will be *un*happy.

This was good news for grandma and grandpa fresh out of the Depression.

But it's bad news for a generation of dreamers marked by off-the-charts high expectations.

My point — and thank you for not giving up a few paragraphs ago — is that we should *expect* our work to be a mixed bag — good *and* bad. We should expect some of our dreams to come true *and* to feel a bit of letdown. We should expect work to give us a sense of meaning and purpose *and* to be regularly frustrated by whatever it is we do.

We can't find happiness or satisfaction or whatever it is that we're searching for in work or in rest, *apart from God*.

That's the bad news.

Here's the good news.

What if God set it up this way?

What if this was all God's idea?

What if he's up to something?

After all, *he* was the one who cursed the ground. We sinned, true, but *he* cursed the ground.

Why would he do that? Why would a loving, generous Creator *curse* his own creation? Is he cruel? Sadistic? Psychopathic? Just plain mean?

Here's my theory; I think the curse is a blessing in camouflage. It's God's love in disguise. His mercy incognito.[14]

Because the curse drives us to God.

If it weren't for the curses — on both the family and the field — we would look to whatever it is we do for work or rest, *and we would find it.* And nothing could be more disastrous for the world than God's image bearers finding identity and belonging and even satisfaction apart from him.

Thankfully, that will never happen.

Whether we look to the family — marriage, childbearing, parenting, relationships, tradition . . .

Or to the field — work, our job, career, what we accomplish or buy or sell . . .

Or even to rest — play, leisure, music, food, drink, vacation, skiing . . .

None of these things — as fantastic as they are — will ever yield the kind of life we crave. At least, not all by themselves.

All these somethings push us to Someone.

And don't think I'm slipping into a dualistic, ascetic worldview, as if we should all abandon our job, go off into the desert and pray 24/7 in a cave. Often we find that Someone in the last place we expect — in our work and in our rest.

Think of the Eden story — God comes to Adam and Eve when they are hiding in the bushes. *Right after* they royally screw up. That's what God is like. He doesn't hang back, arms crossed, mad and withdrawn, and wait for Adam to wise up. No, he comes *to* our first parents, right in the middle of all their mess and failure.

Often we expect to find God where we go *to him* — at church or in prayer or on a retreat. And he's there for sure. He's God. He's everywhere. But he's also where we *least* expect him — at the office, in the meeting that's spiraling out of control, in biology class, in the kitchen, when you're paying off your mountain of debt for that vacation to Kauai — he's there too.

For most of us, the *last* place we expect to find God is at the job we hate. But what if that's one of the first places we should look?

I bet you anything he's there. Doing what he always does — saving us.

In fact, what if our work — even the hard, difficult, frustrating parts of it — are one of, if not the *primary* context where God does his work of salvation? By *salvation* I don't just mean the transition "out of hell and into heaven." Hopefully you know by now that's just the beginning. I mean Jesus remaking us into the people we were supposed to be all along — kings and queens over the world. To get us ready for what's coming.

Because for followers of Jesus, Eden is where we come from, and it's also where we're going.

But before we get to our destination, we need to make one more stop first ...

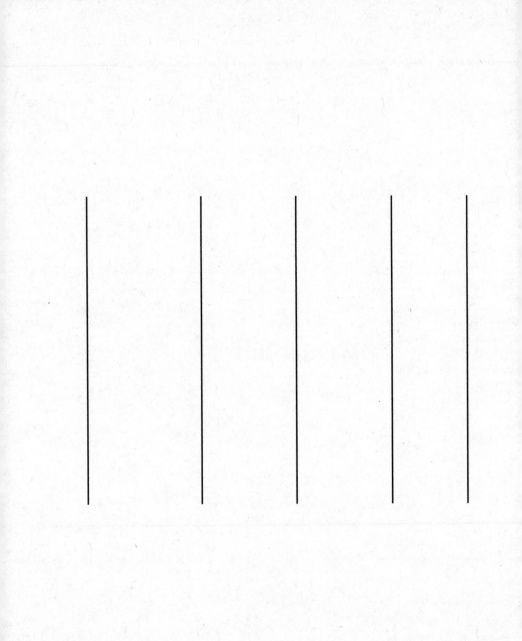

I am not a machine

Bridgetown just about killed me a few years back.

I was twenty-three when we started the church. Who knows anything about *anything* at twenty-three? But from day one God was up to something unique. Lots of people were coming to Jesus, even more people were getting turned inside out by Jesus' way, and the growth was explosive.

Church planting is a cross between a Silicon Valley start-up and D-Day. Let's just say it takes a lot out of you.

The first year was exhausting but exhilarating. I had never been a part of anything like it.

The second year was exhausting but good.

The third year was exhausting. That's it. Just exhausting.

By the fourth year I was *dying* — twenty-seven and on the edge of a nervous breakdown. Stressed out. At the doctor, sick all the time. On edge with my wife. Mad at the world. The campfire was down to a tiny flame and a whole lot of smoke. My heart was just about to give out.

T and I didn't have any kids yet, so I would just work all the time. I would wake up at six every morning, read and pray for a bit, and then work until about ten p.m. *Six days a week.* By the time I got to my day off, there wasn't much left of me. We called it my recovery day. I would sleep through half the morning, and when I got up, I was usually in a foul mood. I spent the day playing catch-up — running errands, paying the bills, to-dos around our loft apartment. Basically I was doing all the work I didn't get paid for. And then we would go shopping and buy stuff. Isn't that what you do after you work for a paycheck? Sometimes we would see a movie, usually we would get in a fight, and then we would go back to sleep. My day off was the worst day of my week, without fail.

You can only live like that for so long until it does something to your soul. You erode away a part of your humanness.

Part of the problem was that I *love* my job. I can blame it on the nature of church work — which is basically a to-do list stretching to infinity and back again, but the reality is I'm a workaholic. I love my job *too* much. I, like a lot of people, was erecting my own Babel, looking to my job for my identity and self-worth. And that road goes straight into the dark and then off a cliff.

So there I was, in my late twenties, starting to burn out, thinking about quitting the job I used to love but didn't anymore, *miserable*, and then I found a little book by a Jewish mystic on the Sabbath.[1] I read it. Then I read it again. Then I read it *again*. I hate to say, This book changed my life! but, well, this book changed my life. For the first time I started to practice the art form of Sabbath, an art form as ancient as creation itself.

In Genesis 2, at the end of the creation story, we read, "Thus the heavens and the earth were completed in all their vast array. By the seventh day God had finished the work he had been doing; so on the seventh day he rested from all his work."[2]

As I said earlier in the book, the creation story starts with God working and ends with God resting. After six "days" of world making, it's done. The universe is "completed."

And you think *your* week was productive?

Then we read that God rested.

Make sure you catch that.

God rested.

God, who doesn't need sleep or a day off or a vacation, who doesn't get tired or worn down or grouchy, who is without parallel to any other being in the universe, *rested*.

And at the risk of sounding like a broken record, I want you to remember that *we are made in his image.* We are made to mirror and mimic what God is like to the world.

God works, so we work.

God rests, so we rest.

Work and rest live in a symbiotic relationship. If you don't learn how to rest well, you will never learn how to work well (and vice versa). After all, the opposite of work isn't rest — it's *sleep*. Work and rest are friends, not enemies. They are a bride and groom who come together to make a full, well-rounded life.

Sabbath isn't just a day to *not work*; it's a day to delight in what one Hebrew poet called "the work of our hands."[3] To delight in the life you've carved out in partnership with God, to delight in the world around you, and to delight in God himself. Sabbath is a day to pull up a chair, sink into it, look back over the work of the last six days, and just *enjoy*.

The word *rested* in Genesis 2 is *shabat* in Hebrew, where we get the word *Sabbath*. It essentially means "to stop" or "cease" or "be complete," but it can also be translated "to celebrate."

Jews have been practicing the art of Sabbath for millennia. We have *a lot* we can learn from them. They talk a lot about *menuha* — another Hebrew word that's translated "rest," but it's a very specific kind of rest. It's not just a nap on the couch. It's a restfulness that's also a celebration. It's often translated "happiness." And to the Jews, *menuha* is something you create. It's not just that you stop working and sit on the couch for a day every week. It's about cultivating an environment, an atmosphere to enjoy your life, your world, and your God. It's more of a mode of being than a twenty-four-hour time slot.

We all need a little *menuha* once in a while. And that's what the Sabbath is for.

The Sabbath is a day when God has my rapt attention.

It's a day when I'm fully available to my family and friends.

The Sabbath is a day with no to-do list. It's a day when I don't accomplish anything, *and I don't feel guilty*.

It's a day when my phone is off, my email is closed, and you can't get ahold of me.

The Sabbath *isn't* a day to buy or sell — to get *more*. It's a day to enjoy what I already have.

It isn't a day to be sad.

Because the Sabbath is a day for *menuha* — for the celebration of life in God's very good world.

After six "days" of universe-sculpting work, God *rested*. And in doing so, he built a rhythm into creation itself. We work for six days, and then we rest for one. And this cadence of work and rest is just as vital to our humanness as food or water or sleep or oxygen. It's mandatory for survival, to say nothing of flourishing. I'm not a machine. I can't work seven days a week. I'm a *human*. All I can do is work for six days and then rest for one, just like the God whose image I bear.

After God rested, we read, "Then God blessed the seventh day and made it holy, because on it he rested from all the work of creating that he had done."**4**

There are two fascinating words here that we need to drill down on: *blessed* and *holy*.

The word *bless* is *barak* in Hebrew, pronounced like the president. A *barak*, or a blessing, in the creation story is a life-giving ability to procreate — to make *more life*.

God *barak*ed three times in *Genesis*.

First, God blessed the "living creatures" (the animal kingdom) and said, "Be fruitful and increase in number. Fill the earth."

Then he blessed human and said the exact same thing, "Be fruitful and increase in number. Fill the earth."

And *then* he "blessed the seventh day."

So he blesses the living creatures.

Then he blesses human.

Then he blesses, *a day*? How does that work?

The Sabbath has a life-giving ability to procreate — to fill the world up with life.

No matter how much you love your job or fine-tune your work/life balance, by the end of the week, you're tired. Your fuel cells are on empty. But rest *refills* us — with energy, creativity, vision, strength, optimism, buoyancy, clarity, and hope. Rest is life-giving.

Because God *barak*ed the Sabbath day.

So that's the first word. One more. Next we read that God made the Sabbath *holy*. In Hebrew, it's this weighty, serious word — *qadosh*. Usually this word is used for God.

God is *qadosh*. He's holy.

The rabbis make a big deal about the "principle of first

mention," which, put simply, means the first time you read a word in the Scriptures it's kind of like a definition. It sets the stage for how you read the word all the way through.

Did you know that the first time you read the word *qadosh* in the Bible is right here? And what does God make holy?

Time.

This is intriguing. You would think that after creating the world, God would make a holy *space* — a mountain or a temple or a shrine. After all, every other religion has a holy space. Islam has Mecca. Hinduism has the Ganges River. Paganism has Stonehenge. Baseball has Wrigley Field.

But this God doesn't have a holy *space*; he has a holy *time* — the Sabbath. This God isn't found in the world of space — in a temple, on top of a mountain, at a spring, around a statue or a monument. He's found in the world of time.

Heschel said, "The Sabbaths are our great cathedrals."[5] There is a hierarchy to time. Not all moments are created equal. Some moments are much, much better than others.

For six days we wrestle with the world of space — the hard work of building civilization. But on the Sabbath, we savor the world of time. We slow down, take a deep breath, and drink it all in.

We push the Slow-Mo button.

Yesterday was the first warm, sunny day of the year — it hit 70. When that happens in Portland, it's like a de facto citywide party. I had a busy day, but there was a brief moment where I was at my house and I had ten minutes to spare before I needed to head out. So I sat on my patio, in the sun, took my shirt off, and just *slowed everything down*. My goal was to make those ten minutes feel like ten hours.

The Sabbath is like that. It's a day where your goal is to savor every second. Because it's holy.

Is this how you think of holiness?

Sadly, a lot of us think of holiness in the negative — about what we *don't* do. We don't get drunk or we don't sleep around or we don't watch R-rated movies (unless they are about Jesus or have Russell Crowe in them). And that's not all bad, but it's one-sided. Holiness also has a positive side. It's about what we *do*.

Later, in *Exodus*, there's a gripping story about Moses and Israel out in the wilderness. They are starving to death, and so God sends this strange new food called manna. It literally falls from the sky every morning, and all they have to do is go out and pick it up. With one exception. On the sixth day *twice* as much falls from the sky. And on the seventh day — the Sabbath — nothing. The sky is empty.

The people are confused when they wake up on day six and there's an extra bag of groceries, so Moses says, "Tomorrow is to be a day of sabbath rest, a holy sabbath to the LORD. So bake what you want to bake and boil what you want to boil. Save whatever is left and keep it until morning."[6]

A holy Sabbath to the LORD.

This language of holy *to* the LORD is used all through the Scriptures. It can also be translated *"dedicated* to the LORD." So the Sabbath is an entire day that is holy, set aside, dedicated *to* the LORD.

It's a day for rest, *and* it's a day for worship.

When I Sabbath, I run everything through this grid — is this rest? Is this worship? If the answer to both questions is yes, then I delight in it; if the answer is no, then I hold off until the next day.

Because the Sabbath is not the same thing as a day off.

Make sure you get the difference.

On a day off you don't work for your employer, but you still work. You grocery shop, go to the bank, mow the lawn, work on the remodel project, chip away at that sci-fi novel you're writing . . .

On the Sabbath, you rest, and you worship. That's it.

That's why Moses was teaching the Israelites to get ready for the Sabbath. To bake and boil and gear up for the day of rest. Think of the Sabbath like a weekly holiday. You don't just wake up on Christmas morning and think, *What should we do today?* No, you *get ready* for it. The same is true for Thanksgiving or the Fourth of July or your birthday or anniversary — you plan and prep and shop and look forward to it for days at a time.[7] In my family, we Sabbath from Friday at sundown through Saturday, so Friday afternoons are always a flurry of activity. We clean the house and finish the to-do list and stop by the market and plan out the day ahead, and then finally, *it comes.*

Blessed and holy.

Here's what I'm saying: there is a rhythm to this world. For six days we rule and subdue and work and draw out and labor and bleed and wrestle and fight with the ground. But then we take a step back, and for twenty-four hours, we *sabbath*, we enjoy the fruit of our labor, we delight in God and his world, we celebrate life, we rest, and we worship.

The Creator God is inviting us to join him in this rhythm, this interplay of work and rest. And when we don't accept his invitation, we reap the consequences. Fatigue. Burnout. Anxiety. Depression. Busyness. Starved relationships. Worn-down immune systems. Low energy levels. Anger. Tension. Confusion. Emptiness. These are the signs of a life without rest.

Maybe that's why later the Sabbath is *commanded*. When Israel is at the base of Mount Sinai, God comes down on top of the mountain in a cloud of fire and smoke and lightning. And then with a voice like a California earthquake, God speaks the Ten Commandments over his people. His vision for humanness is shrunk down to *ten* commands — so few a child can count them on their fingers.

And guess what the longest, most in-depth command is?

The Sabbath. It gets more real estate than any of the others.

God starts off by saying, "Remember the Sabbath day."[8]

So the Sabbath is something that's easy to forget. It's easy to get sucked into this 24/7, go-go-go, hamster wheel that we call the modern world. We're to *remember* the Sabbath.

How? By "keeping it holy."

So the Sabbath *is* holy, but it's also something we have to *keep* holy. It's easy to profane, to desecrate. It's easy for it to just become another day in the rat race. Another day to fall into the pattern — work, buy, sell, repeat. We're to *keep it holy* — to guard it, watch over it, treat it like a delicate flower in a New York subway.

If you're thinking, *Why should I go to all this trouble?* God ends his longest commandment with the answer, "For in six days the LORD made the heavens and the earth, the sea, and all that is in them, but he rested on the seventh day. Therefore the LORD blessed the Sabbath day and made it holy."

So, for God, his Sabbath commandment is grounded in the creation story itself.

Lots of people argue that we're "free" from the Sabbath because it was a part of the Torah, or Law. As if it was a legalistic rule we were stuck with until Jesus. What a tragic misunderstanding.

It is true that we're no longer under the Torah, and it's also true that the Sabbath is the only one of the Ten Commandments not repeated in the New Testament.[9] But even so, the Sabbath still stands as wisdom.

There isn't a command in the New Testament to eat food or drink water or sleep eight hours a night. That's just wisdom, how the Creator set up the human body and the world itself.

You can skip the Sabbath — it's not sin. It's just stupid.

You can eat concrete — it's not sin. It's just dumb.

You can stay awake for days at a time like Josh Lyman in *The*

West Wing. Go ahead. God's not mad at you. But if you do that long enough, you'll *die.*

At one point, Moses calls the Sabbath a gift.[10] That's exactly what it is.

I cringe when I hear people argue about whether or not we have to keep the Sabbath, and if so, on what day. Some say Saturday like the Jews, others say Sunday because of Jesus' resurrection, others think any day is fine. But all this arguing is an exercise in *missing the point.* The point is that there is a way the Creator set the creation up to thrive. A way that God set *you* up to thrive. And when we Sabbath, we tap into God's rhythm for human flourishing.

Technically, the Sabbath is from twenty minutes before sundown on Friday evening to Saturday late afternoon (the Jewish day is measured from sunset to sunset). But most followers of Jesus Sabbath on Sunday, as it's the day of Messiah's resurrection, as well as the day we come together for worship. For me Sunday is a workday. And it's exhausting. I'm up early, gearing up for a marathon day. My last teaching is at eight *p.m.*! So by the time I get home around eleven o'clock, I'm crawling along the floor.

Not literally. That was a metaphor.

So we follow the tradition of Friday night to Saturday late afternoon, but only because it works for our life. I don't think what day you take is important. *Genesis* doesn't say Friday or Saturday; it just says the seventh. And the writer Paul said, "One person considers one day more sacred than another; another considers every day alike. Each of them should be fully convinced in their own mind."[11] I guess people have been arguing about this for a while. For us, Friday night to Saturday just works great.

And for us, the Sabbath is *by far* the highlight of the week. My two youngest children, Moses and Sunday, are both five, so they honestly have no clue how to tell time. Tomorrow and three days from now and next week all blend into one. So *every morning* they ask me, Is it Sabbath? with a big, hopeful, childlike grin. Jude is nine and pretty snappy with his new watch, so he counts down all week long. Three days until Sabbath. Two days left. Tomorrow! Which comes as no surprise. In *Genesis*, Sabbath is the climax of the seven-day cycle. It's on day *seven*, not three or four. It's not a pause so we can recoup and then "get back to work." If anything, it's the other way around. It's the end goal, what the entire week is moving toward. The climax is an entire day set aside to worship.

Just like work, when it's done right, is an act of worship, the same is true with rest. You can rest as an act of worship to God.

You can even rest to the glory of God. When you enjoy the world as God intended — with a cup of coffee, a nap in a hammock, a good meal, time with friends, it glorifies God — it calls attention to the Creator's presence and beauty all around us. And when you do all that in a spirit of gratitude, letting the goodness of your world and life conjure up an awareness of God and a love for him, then rest becomes worship.

Even though the Sabbath is about imitation of the God who works and then rests, it's also a day to remember that *we're not God*. We take a day off, and the world gets along just fine without us.

We're not as important as we think.

The Sabbath is a day to embrace this reality, to let it sink in, to own it, to celebrate it. To celebrate our weakness, our mortality, our *limits*. To celebrate our God of strength and immortality and limitless power. To rest *with* him and to rest *in* him.

That's why Sabbath is an expression of faith. Faith that there is a Creator and he's *good*. We are his creation. This is his world. We live under his roof, drink his water, eat his food, breathe his oxygen. So on the Sabbath, we don't just take a day off from work; we take a day off from *toil*. We give him all our fear and anxiety and stress and worry. We let go. We stop ruling and subduing, and we just *be*. We "remember" our place in the universe. So that we never forget . . .

There is a God, *and I'm not him.*

The anti-Pharaoh

Okay, stay with me. We're just scratching the surface on a theology of Sabbath. Next comes the really good part.

We left off in the last chapter with Moses on Mount Sinai and the now famous Ten Commandments. But the Scriptures have a lot more to say about the seventh day.

If you've been around the church for a while, the odds are you've heard the word *Torah*. Usually when people talk about the Torah, they mean the first five books of the Bible —

Genesis,

Exodus,

Leviticus,

Numbers,

and *Deuteronomy.*

The Ten Commandments are just the beginning of the Torah. All in all there are *613* commandments. They get a bad rap as rules, but in reality they're more like a manifesto for how Israel was to live as the people of God.

Now, the odds are you already know that. But here's something you might not know: Really, there are *two* Torahs.[1]

The first is from Mount Sinai, and it's what we read in *Exodus* and *Leviticus.* This is a generation fresh out of Egypt, with the mud from the brick-pits still in between their toes. God is speaking from the top of the mountain, laying out a vision for how to be human in his new world. But sadly, they botch it. Royally. They don't obey his commandments, instead they relive the old, tired, uncreative story of Adam and Eve all over again — they sin. And so instead of going straight from Egypt to God's new land, they wander. In the desert. *For forty years.* Until they all die off.

Every

last

one.

This is what happens when God's people sin — when we ignore or shrug off or flat-out reject his Torah, his teaching. When we do our own thing.

We wander. In the desert. We end up with a broken GPS and a nasty sunburn.

It's no way to live, much less die.

Anyways, back to Israel. Four decades later, the first generation is all gone, and a new generation is ready to step into the land. The future is a bright white canvas. They are right on the cusp of something amazing.

That's when *Deuteronomy* was written.[2] The name *Deuteronomy* is from two Greek words: *Deutero* meaning "second" and *nomos* meaning "law." It can be translated "the second law" or "the second Torah." It's essentially a sermon. Moses, who's now an elderly man, just days away from his death, is retelling the Torah to this young, green, neophyte generation. And like most elderly men, he's retelling stories we already know, specifically the story of Mount Sinai.

And so we get two versions of the Ten Commandments. One in Exodus 20, and then a second in Deuteronomy 5. They are almost identical.

Almost.

They start exactly the same, "Observe the Sabbath day by keeping it holy, as the LORD your God has commanded you. Six days you shall labor and do all your work, but the seventh day is a sabbath to the LORD your God. On it you shall not do any work, neither you, nor your son or daughter, nor your male or female servant, nor your ox, your donkey or any of your animals, nor any foreigner residing in your towns, so that your male and female servants may rest, as you do."[3]

So, for those of you who really want to force your ox to work seven days a week, I'm sorry — call me a legalistic jerk, but you just can't. Not an option.

Now, in both commands, the first part is indistinguishable. Practically verbatim. But they *end* on a very different note.

At Mount Sinai, it's "for in six days the LORD made the heavens and the earth, the sea, and all that is in them, but he rested on the seventh day. Therefore the LORD blessed the Sabbath day and made it holy."

So at Sinai, the Sabbath command is rooted in the story of creation. We rest because God rests.

But in *Deuteronomy* it ends like this: "Remember that you were slaves in Egypt and that the LORD your God brought you out of there with a mighty hand and an outstretched arm. Therefore the LORD your God has commanded you to observe the Sabbath day."[4]

This is a new twist. Here, nothing is said about creation. Instead, the Sabbath command is grounded in the story of the exodus.

At Sinai, the Sabbath is an art form. It's about tapping into the rhythm of creation; in *Deuteronomy*, the Sabbath is an act of defiance against Pharaoh and his slave drivers.

At Sinai it's a way of saying *yes* to God and his world; in *Deuteronomy* it's a way of saying *no* to Egypt and its system.

At Sinai it's an invitation to join God in his delight; in *Deuteronomy* it's a warning to stay away from Egypt's way of life.

I was first exposed to this way of thinking by the Old Testament scholar Walter Brueggeman, and it was so eye-opening.

Why in the world would Moses need to warn ex-slaves not to go back to slavery?

Because Israel was prone to amnesia. We all are. It's easy to forget the past. And so the Sabbath is a memorial. At Sinai it looks back to Eden, but in *Deuteronomy* it looks back to Egypt.

And Egypt is somewhere you never want to go back to.

In Egypt the Hebrews were slaves. Slaves don't get a Sabbath. Slaves are something less than human. A commodity to buy and sell. They only have value in what they produce. They work all day, every day, until they die.

Rest isn't an option for a slave. Rest is a by-product of freedom. No freedom, no rest.

Language about endless work and restlessness is strung all through the *Exodus* story.

"Why are you taking the people away from their labor? Get back to your work!"[5]

"You are stopping them from working."[6]

"Make the work harder for the people so that they keep working."[7]

"Then the slave drivers and the overseers went out and said to the people, 'This is what Pharaoh says: "I will not give you any more straw. Go and get your own straw wherever you can find it, but your work will not be reduced at all." ' "[8]

"The slave drivers kept pressing them, saying, 'Complete the work required of you for each day, just as when you had straw.' "[9]

"Pharaoh said, 'Lazy, that's what you are — lazy! That is why you keep saying, "Let us go and sacrifice to the LORD". Now get to work. You will not be given any straw, yet you must produce your full quota of bricks.' "[10]

(By the way, this is just from *one chapter.*)

Pharaoh is implacable and relentless. This quasi-divine image of the sun god Re is a tyrant. Ruthless and cruel. No matter how much you produce, *it's never enough*. You live under the ominous shadow of the daily quota —

more,

more,

more!

And it wasn't just Pharaoh screaming for more and more. It was the economic system of Egypt as a whole. Israel wasn't just making bricks; they were making bricks to build supply cities.[11] Entire cities for Pharaoh and his oligarchy to store their *extra* stuff.

Egypt's appetite was rapacious, insatiable. There was never enough bread, enough wine, enough goods, enough services, enough bricks — it was a system of *more*.

And it was a system built on the back of slavery.

To get to the lavish, opulent, hedonistic lifestyle of Pharaoh, you have to stand on the backs of cheap labor, which is a nice way of saying slavery. It's ironic that when economists draw out a diagram for the global economy it looks *exactly* like Pharaoh's pyramids. For a dinky minority to live Egypt's lifestyle, wait, I mean America's lifestyle, it takes the masses at the bottom, working for next to nothing. Cheap labor means cheap clothing, cheap food, cheap goods and services, cheap gas, cheap technology, and so on.

Slavery sounds a lot like 30 percent off.

Think of the saying, "This shirt was a *steal*." It's unnerving how accurate that statement is. Everything we enjoy costs something. And if it doesn't cost us, it costs someone else.

Pharaoh is alive and well.

He's that guilty feeling in your gut, that voice in the back of your head, screaming at you, "Work harder, work faster, work longer. Produce, produce, produce. You're only as good as your daily quota. Make more bricks!"

His psychological abuse is like waterboarding for the mind.

And it's not just Pharaoh's ghost haunting our world. His economic system is still thriving. We don't call it Egypt anymore. We call it "capitalism" or "free trade" or "consumerism" or "Black Friday" or "0.7 percent financing." And it's ubiquitous. You can't drive down the road or stand in a grocery-store line or open your computer without Egypt screaming at you, Get more, own more, have more! Who cares where it comes from? Who cares what it costs those below you? You work hard. You deserve it. You don't have *enough*.

Now, I'm not anti-American. I have no problem saying I'm a capitalist, not a Marxist. But seriously, it's getting ridiculous out there.

Israel isn't the only one prone to amnesia. Some of us *want* to go back to Egypt. We miss it there. After all, Egypt is lousy if you're a Hebrew, but it's really nice if you're an Egyptian.

There's a little bit of Pharaoh in all of us. Our endless desire for *more*. And with our endless desire comes *restlessness*.

Remember how I said that before I started taking a Sabbath, my day off was the worst day of my week? I realized later that one of the many reasons I hated my day off was because I was addicted to the drug of production. The stimulating, titillating sensation you get from accomplishment and accumulation. There's nothing like the feeling of getting stuff *done*.

On my day off I would go through withdrawals. I would feel *guilty* — no matter how hard I worked that week, I would hear Pharaoh's voice in my head, "Lazy, lazy." The temptation to just check my email or text that guy back or pop into the office for a minute or get ahead on my teaching for the weekend — it was overwhelming. Homer's sirens have nothing on Egypt's gravitational pull.

And it wasn't just my desire to *produce* more, but also to *get* more. If I wasn't tempted to check my email, I was tempted to go shopping. I was the oppressed and the oppressor, slave and slave driver. I was back in Pharaoh's Egypt.

The Sabbath is about leaving Egypt behind. About emancipation from Pharaoh's suffocating rule. It's about freedom.

Americans are working more than ever before. One study I read recently said that from 1973 to 1990 the average work-week went up from 41 hours to 47 hours. And that's not too bad, but over the same time period the amount of time spent on rest went down *37 percent*!

This is due in large part to technology. So-called "labor-saving devices" have actually skyrocketed the amount of hours we work. You used to have to go into the office or to the jobsite to work. Now all you have to do is reach over and grab your phone off your bedside table.

Remember about a decade ago when the Blackberry first hit the market? (For those of you who are younger, I know it's hard to imagine a pre-iPhone world. It was rough.) People called it the "Crackberry," and there was all this dialogue about the dangers of working all hours of the day and night and being connected 24/7. People were doing crazy things like checking their email at the dinner table or from the couch in the living room.

Insane, I know.

Why isn't anybody talking about that anymore? Just to clarify, *it's worse than ever.* I think an armistice was called because the Amish didn't stand a chance against the global military-industrial complex that is Apple, Twitter, and friends (he said sarcastically as he was typing on his MacBook Pro and tweeting every few hours).

We need to start talking about technology. I'm not Amish. Technology does a *ton* of good. I'm actually from Silicon Valley. But that said, there are *sins* of technology.

Every generation has its blind spots. I'm starting to realize this is one of ours.

We need to relearn how to power down, unplug, disconnect, take a break, and *be in one place at one time.* We forget that we're not a machine. We can't work 24/7.

In a world of workaholism and nonstop technology and Amazon.com drone delivery and the unending barrage of consumerism, *and* in a world of opulent waste and leisure and the revision of the American dream to mean golfing in Florida all day long or driving your Maserati around Beverly Hills — recalibrating our life to the rhythm of work and rest is more important than ever before. Both underwork and overwork rob us of the capacity to enjoy God and his world. They make us less *human.*

So, we *work* more than ever before, and we *have* more than ever before.

We make up over 22 percent of the global economy, even though we only have 4 percent of the world's population.[12] California alone puts out over 2 *trillion* dollars a year — that's more than the entire GDP of Italy. And California has 37 percent fewer *people* than the land of pasta and expensive fashion. One economist gave this explanation, "That's a testament to the superior, world-class productivity of the American worker."[13] Uh-huh. That's one way to put it.

Since 1950 the per capita income of Americans has *tripled*. The average size of an American home has gone up by almost a thousand square feet, from about 1,300 to 2,300. But the average size of the family has been *cut in half* — from 4.32 to 2.58.

Seriously, who has 4.32 kids anymore?[14]

But in spite of all this exponential growth, we're as unhappy as ever. In fact, we're worse. We spend about 250 billion dollars a year on prescription drugs. Antidepressants are the second most popular prescription in the US, after cholesterol medication. One in 10 people are on antidepressants at any given time. More like 1 in 4 over a lifetime.[15] Mental illness is exploding. Bipolar disorder, schizophrenia, ADHD — they are up by a staggering amount.[16]

Abraham Heschel was spot-on when he said, "There is happiness in the love of labor, there is misery in the love of gain."[17]

So, to sum up . . .

We *work* more than ever before,

we *have* more than ever before,

and we're miserable.

It's Egypt all over again.

This is why Moses is calling Israel to remember that they were slaves in Egypt. What an odd command, right? Slaves don't forget they were slaves any more than vets from Iraq forget they went through hell. The African American slave trade was more than two centuries ago, but it's still fresh in our minds, an open wound in our culture. And it should be. It was horrific.

The command isn't just to remember they were slaves, but to remember they *were* slaves. As in, they *aren't* anymore. That, sadly, is easy to forget.

Just like Israel, we forget that Pharaoh is dead. There are no more slave drivers. No more quota. We're free. We don't have to work seven days a week. Our value is no longer tied to what we accomplish. The goal of work isn't to make money to buy more stuff; it's to cooperate with the Creator God in world making, and then to take a step back and delight in our Garden-like world.

Sabbath is an act of resistance to Pharaoh and his system. Egypt's cycle of brick making and supply-city building is unending. Sabbath is a way to break the addictive pattern of accomplish more, accumulate more, repeat. It's an act of defiance and rebellion against the endless, restless grind of workaholism and consumerism.

Sabbath is a way to say *ENOUGH!*

Enough work. Work is a good thing, but it's not *the* thing. There's more to life than production. There's pleasure. Sabbath is a way to break our addiction to accomplishment. One day a week we cease *all* work — not just the work we get paid for. We rest even from the *thought* of labor.

Enough stuff. We don't need any more than we already have. Sabbath is a way to break our addiction to accumulation. Do we really need *another* pair of shoes?

Now, stuff isn't all bad — we don't want to slip into dualism here. God created the world, and he called it very good. Food, drink, a place to call home, clothing to wear, a car to drive — these are not bad things. But the problem is that we always want *more* of them.

Psychologists have this phrase, "the hedonic treadmill," which, put simply, is the idea that the more you get the more you want. Hedonism — the good life — is a treadmill. It's like we're always moving forward but never getting anywhere. We never arrive. We never feel like we have *enough*. Consumerism is a thief, a bandit. It takes more than it gives. Because for every one thing you get, there are ten more things you discover you want.

This happens to be me every January, right after Christmas. I get all this stuff — mostly clothing. But then I realize all the stuff I still don't have. So I get a pair of jeans, but I need a new pair of shoes to go with my jeans, which means I need a new belt to match, because mine is black and my new shoes are brown. But while I'm at it, I might as well get a new shirt, 'cause I really could use one, and when I'm at the menswear shop I notice this watch … and we're back on the hamster wheel.

Sabbath is a line in the sand. A shot across the bow. "This far you shall go and no further." No more work, no more stuff, no *more*.

Enough is enough.

I do not have to work more.

I do not have to buy more.

I do not have to sell more.

I do not have to move up in the company.

I do not have to earn my Father's love.

I don't have anything to prove.

I do not have to get a perfect score.

I do not need another stamp on my passport.

I do not need another bay in my garage.

I do not need to be younger or more beautiful or have flatter abs (although, man, that would be nice).

I don't need to have my kids in ballet or soccer *all year long*.

I don't need to make everybody happy.

I don't need to get everything I want.

There is no quota. The only slave drivers are the ones in my head. My value doesn't come from what I produce, and my joy and peace don't rise and fall with my net worth. Pharaoh is dead. Egypt is in the past. I'm not a slave anymore.

I'm free.

And I'm a part of a different kingdom now, with a different king.

Sabbath is an act of resistance to Pharaoh, *and* it's an act of alignment with YHWH, the God of Israel.[18]

YHWH is not a workaholic. He's a Sabbath-keeping, Sabbath-giving, Sabbath-commanding God. A God who works, and a God who *rests*.

Sabbath is a way to say *yes* to YHWH. To silence Pharaoh's voice and break free from Egypt's pull and to tune our life to YHWH, the rest-God. It's a way to *remember* and never forget that what we're craving, and even coveting, isn't found in the world of space, but in the world of time — in God himself. This isn't to devalue the world of space. No, this world is good. It's just to put it in its proper place. The world and all the stuff in it are gifts to enjoy, not gods to worship.

That's what idolatry is — the human quest to take the divine and reduce it to a commodity — something made out of wood or stone, something you can buy and sell, something you can own or have (and, as a result, lose). Idolatry is when we look to the creation for something we can only get from the Creator. But God isn't a commodity. He's a Spirit. Intangible but real. Invisible but true. He doesn't have an idol. The closest thing he has is *us*, his image bearers.

And to YHWH, we're not cheap labor. We're partners.

There's no quota, no supply cities. There's a Garden.

YHWH is nothing like Pharaoh. He's a lot more like Jesus ...

The Lord of the Sabbath

For Jesus, the Sabbath was a day to get in trouble.

He was a bit of a rabble-rouser. A gadfly. The Son of Man had a mischievous side. You don't get crucified for being a people pleaser.

In story after story, in all four gospels, Jesus is tangling with the Pharisees — this uptight, right-wing group of religious conservatives — over the Sabbath. And the crux of the debate was over healing on the Sabbath. Is it okay to heal on the seventh day? Or *not*? Put another way, is healing work? Or rest?

The biographer Mark tells this story about Jesus and his disciples walking through a cornfield on the Sabbath. The disciples "began to pick some ears of corn" — the first-century equivalent of snacking. The Pharisees, meanwhile, are snooping around, watching Jesus from a distance. When they see the disciples eating corn, they say to Jesus, "Look, why are they doing what is unlawful on the Sabbath?"[1]

Unlawful?

So snacking was against the law?

Well, there's no law against picking ears of corn in the Torah. All the Torah says is "On (the Sabbath) you shall not do any work."[2] But that's a little bit ambiguous, right? I mean, what exactly *is* work? It's harder to define than you would think.

And it's even more frustrating to define *rest*.

Take exercise for example. I'm a runner. Is running work or rest? For some people running is life-giving, as helpful as a therapy session, and it's free. But for other people, it's a cross between Guantanamo Bay and a root canal.

What about gardening? I hate it. I love healthy, whole natural local food, of course, but I want somebody *else* to grow it. But I know a lot of people who *love* to garden. For them, it's soothing.

What about cooking? Taking a shower? Going on a walk? Playing the piano? Is that work or rest?

It's unclear. Some stuff is clearly work — like going into the office or framing a house or doing laundry, and some stuff is clearly rest — like sleeping or relaxing in a hammock or reading a book you love. But there's a whole lot of stuff that falls into the nebulous middle. So, where it's unclear, ask the follow-up question, Is this life-giving? If it feels like rest for you, and if it feels like worship, then go for it.

Now, this kind of freedom and space and elasticity drives Pharisees crazy. Pharisees are rule people. (I would know, I'm one of them.) We think of the Pharisees as evil, mean bigots, and to an extent they were, but they started out with good hearts. They were born in the exile — when Israel was in Babylon. Even when Israel came back home to Jerusalem, they were quickly conquered again. By Jesus' day they were under Rome's oppressive rule. They were back in the land, but they were still in exile. And everybody knew they were in exile for breaking God's commandments. So the Pharisees' basic philosophy was this: if Torah-breaking got us into this mess, then it stands to reason that Torah-keeping will get us out of it. So they were OCD about the Torah.

To make sure they didn't break any commandments on acci-dent, they did something called "building a fence around the Torah." They would take a commandment in the Torah, like "Remember the Sabbath day by keeping it holy" — and they would add on extra commands — they would build a fence around it, just to make sure they didn't break it on accident.

As I'm writing this I'm over on the Oregon Coast, in this little town I love called Pacific City. Right outside my door is Cape Kiwanda, a natural rock formation rising hundreds of feet into the air and jutting out into the Pacific. It's my favorite place in Oregon. If you climb up to the top of the cape, there's a sign that reads, "Danger! Stay away from the edge." *And* there's a fence about ten feet from the edge of the cliff, just in case you don't see the sign. Now, seeing as I'm not the kind of guy who would *ever* climb over the fence and walk right up to the edge, I have no idea what that fence is there for . . .

In a similar way, the Pharisees took the commandment "Remember the Sabbath day," and they built a fence around it. They added on dozens and dozens of rules. They broke down "work" into thirty-nine categories. How far you could walk, how much weight you could carry, what you could cook, and so on.

By the time of Jesus there was the written law of the Torah, with its 613 commandments. Plus, on *top* of that was the oral law called the Mishnah, and there were an extra 1,500 rules in it. *1,500!*

Some people really like rules.

When the Pharisees ask why the disciples are doing something that is "unlawful," they don't mean the disciples are breaking the Torah; they would never do that. They are breaking the Mishnah. But to Jesus, the Mishnah was just rules on top of rules — some good, some not-so-good, but all made up by men, not from God.

Jesus' answer is profound. After retelling a story about King David and his men eating bread from the house of God, he says this:

"The Sabbath was made for man, not man for the Sabbath. So the Son of Man is Lord even of the Sabbath."

Lots of people misread Jesus here. We read all these stories where Jesus is fighting with the Pharisees over the Sabbath, and it's easy to think Jesus is down on the Sabbath. As if the Sabbath is legalistic, or it's part of the Law. But keep in mind that the Sabbath predates the Law by thousands of years. It's more of a rhythm in creation than a rule in a book.

The reality is the Sabbath is un-American, inconvenient, and we want an excuse to write it off.

Jesus isn't down on the Sabbath. But somewhere along the way, the Pharisees lost the plotline. They lost sight of what the Sabbath is all about. They got out of sync with God's heart. And Jesus is calling them back to the Sabbath's roots.

The Sabbath is more of an art form than a list of dos and don'ts. Yes, there are rules. Some rules are healthy. "Drive on the right side of the road" is a *great* rule (unless you're in

England). "Don't play with fire" is another great rule. Some rules are life-giving.

So on the Sabbath, in my family, we have rules.

We do ...

Sleep in.

Relax.

Spend time in the Scriptures.

Pray.

Eat our way through the day.

Enjoy nature — go for a walk, to the park, or sometimes on a light hike.

Spend time with close friends and family.

We don't ...

Buy or sell (except for food, as we love to go out for brunch or ice cream).

Touch our email.

Post anything on social media (because our phones are *off*).

Run errands or catch up around the house.

Talk about stuff that's heavy or sad or divisive — there are six *other* days in the week for that.

Talk about stuff we need to get done. We rest from even the *thought* of work.

Read a magazine or visit a website or go to a store that would make me want *more* — because on the Sabbath, we have enough.

But these "rules" aren't suffocating or rigid; they are pliable and limber and spacious. They are the rules of a craft, a discipline, an art form.

After all, *shabat* is a verb in Genesis 2. Rest is something you *do*. It's a skill you hone. And just like surfing or cooking or playing the oboe, nobody is good at it the first time. It takes time and practice.

Maybe this Sabbath conversation is all new for you. I hope and pray that after reading this book, you start to Sabbath. It honestly changed my life, and I think it has the potential to do the same for you. But just to give you a heads-up, it might be a little rough at first. It might feel odd, weird, even frustrating.

A few years ago I started racing in triathlons. This guy in our church, Brian, was a former professional triathlete. He has a body like a Greek god and was kind enough to train me (sadly, I *don't* have a body like a Greek god). The main thing he taught me was to change the cadence of my run from long, slow, heavy strides to short, quick, light strides. And then he trained me to match my running stride to my cycling stride, so that when I get off the bike, I just *keep going*. As easy as that sounds, it was *so* hard to change. Learning a new rhythm is never easy, but it's worth the effort.

Brian had a lot of rules — chin up, run on the balls of your feet, straight back, eyes forward, arms at a slight angle, and so on. But he wasn't a legalistic jerk; he was a trainer. He wanted me to get in the best shape of my life and swim, cycle, and run *better*.

See what I'm getting at?

First-century Jews needed to hear the second part of Jesus teaching: "The Sabbath was made for man, *not man for the Sabbath*." They had it backward. The Sabbath isn't a cold, arbitrary rule we have to obey. It's a life-giving art form that we get to practice.

But I would argue that twenty-first-century Americans need to hear the *first* part of Jesus' teaching: "*The Sabbath was made for man*." It's not that we have too many rules about the Sabbath, it's that we don't have *any at all*. The vast majority of us don't even take a Sabbath. We love our "time off." We take a weekend, a holiday, a vacation. We love to play, and that's great. But very few of us actually take a *Sabbath* — a day for nothing more than rest and worship.

That's why we need to take a closer look at the stories about Jesus and the Sabbath. In fact, this one's not over yet. After his pithy line about how the Sabbath was made for man, Jesus goes into the synagogue to teach. The synagogue was where you would usually find Jesus on the Sabbath — with God's people. This Saturday morning, a man was there with a deformed hand. Now, Jesus is on thin ice with the Pharisees. Mark writes, "Some of them were looking for a reason to accuse Jesus, so they watched him closely to see if he would heal him on the Sabbath."

But Jesus is never one to shy away from a fight. He said to the sick man, "Stand up in front of everyone." So whatever it is that Jesus is about to do, he wants it done for all to see — no sleight of hand. This one is on display.

Then he said, "Stretch out your hand." The guy stretched it out, and "his hand was completely restored." This was a flagrant, in-your-face, stick-it-to-the-man act of defiance. Which is why "the Pharisees went out and began to plot with the Herodians how they might kill Jesus."

Seriously, religious people are insane.

Now, as I said earlier, it's easy to misread stories like this, as if the main point is the Sabbath is a bad, legalistic rule that we have to abandon. That's missing the heart of the story.

Jesus was known far and wide as a healer. Healing is a tangible expression of the in-breaking kingdom of God. But did you know that almost all of Jesus' healings take place on the Sabbath?

I don't think that's a coincidence.

Why? Because *the Sabbath is a day for healing.*

That was true in the first century, and I would argue it's true today.

Jesus does some of his best work on the Sabbath. Which is fitting. The Sabbath is all about intimacy with God. And healing is a sign of God's love for you. What better time for Jesus to heal than on the Sabbath?

The reality is that we all get beat up by life. I'm a pastor, but sometimes I feel like a prizefighter. By the end of the week, I'm not just tired, I'm sore, raw, achy, swollen, and worn down.

The Sabbath comes to my door like a doctor, or should I say *the Lord of the Sabbath* comes like a doctor to patch me up.

So I have my rules, but all I'm doing is creating an environment where it's easy for Jesus to do his healing work,

week

after week

after week.

Now, at the risk of squelching your creativity, here's what a Sabbath looks like for me. I hesitate to write this because there's no right way to Sabbath. There's wisdom, yes, but all sorts of room to breathe. What's life-giving for an introvert-reader-dad-of-three might not be for an extrovert-college-student-Instagrammer or a middle-age couple or an astronaut at the International Space Station (just in case you're up there and you're reading this book, ya know . . .). That said, here's what a Sabbath looks like for me.

As I said earlier, the day before, Friday, is what the writer John called "the day of Preparation."[3] We gear up, shop, plan, clean, finish up — like we're getting ready for a holiday. It's like having Christmas once a week. The last few hours of Friday afternoon are always a bit stressful but mixed with a lot of anticipation.

Right before Sabbath starts, I walk through my pre-Sabbath ritual. I go into my home office, clear off my desk, put away my to-do list, power down my computer, turn off my phone, and put it all in the closet.

Then twenty minutes before sunset, we all circle up in the living room as a family. We follow a few ancient Sabbath traditions: Tammy and the kids light the candles of Sabbath. I pour the wine (don't worry, grape juice for the kids) for the *kiddush*, an ancient blessing. We read a psalm and then say a prayer to invite the Spirit of Jesus to take us into a posture of rest and worship.

Then we *eat*. A lot. Dinner was made earlier in the day, so all we have to do is set it on the table and dig in. We take our time. Talk about the highlight of the week. Have friends or family over. Have seconds. Dessert. More wine.

It's *so* good.

Then after dinner we relax. Read. Sit by the fire in the winter. Go for a walk in the summer. Before I put the kids to bed, I read to them from the Scriptures.

Tammy and I usually spend some, ya know, "quality time" together and go to bed early. We call it reverse sleeping in. My body is in a rhythm now, so by nine p.m. on Friday night, I'm making my way toward bed. There's no TV or anything digital, so the house is quiet and at peace.

I am quiet and at peace.

Saturday morning I wake up — *whenever I want*. I'm not a morning person, so it's usually not that early. I just let my body wake up when it wants to. But after going to bed so early, I feel like a new man.

After I greet my family, I make coffee (Chemex, naturally) and go into my study to read. I start in the Psalms, then Jesus in the Gospels, then the Old Testament, then the New Testament. I take my time. I'm not in a rush. I think, pray, *listen*. Usually I read a chapter from Heschel's *The Sabbath* before I come out.

When I'm done, I get my three kids on the couch. We drink hot cocoa and read some more from the Scriptures. Then we say a prayer, asking God's grace over the day.

I used to do some light exercise but not anymore. I just *rest*.

After a shower we put on some nice threads and walk to brunch or donuts at Blue Star down the street. We order *whatever* we want. We eat our way through the Sabbath, and when it comes to diet, anything goes. After brunch we come home. The kids go down for a nap. T usually goes on a bike ride to get coffee with a friend. I take a few hours to get my introvert on. I read and journal and think about the week behind me and the week ahead of me. Usually, most of my afternoon is spent on the couch with a novel.

Later, I play Legos with the kids or walk them down to the park or whatever sounds life-giving at the time.

Then as the day winds down, we go on what my son Moses

calls "a praying walk." We just saunter around the neighborhood and thank God for the last twenty-four hours of peace. By the time I'm walking back up the stairs to our house, I'm already looking forward to the *next* Sabbath.

And every week, as the day unfolds, something strange and mystic happens. Right around nine or ten in the morning, *I get my soul back.*

What is that? Is it the Sabbath? Just the nourishing effect of sleep and down time and good food and no to-do list? Or is it something more? Is it the Lord of the Sabbath?

Yes.

It's both.

It was Jesus who said — and this is Eugene Peterson's paraphrase — "Are you tired? Worn out? Burned out on religion? Come to me. Get away with me and you'll recover your life. I'll show you how to take a real rest. Walk with me and work with me — watch how I do it. Learn the unforced rhythms of grace. I won't lay anything heavy or ill-fitting on you. Keep company with me and you'll learn to live freely and lightly."[4]

Jesus is the embodiment of the Sabbath. He's the seventh day in flesh and blood. We can come to him and find *rest*, not just on the Sabbath, but all week long.

Old Testament scholar Walter Brueggemann said, "People who keep Sabbath live all seven days differently."[5] Sabbath isn't just a Pause button — it's a full, complete, total system restart. We power down, cool off, let the fan wind down, and then reboot. Sabbath is a chance to take a long, hard look at our lives and to retune them to the right key. To make sure that our life is shaped around what really matters. And when we see stuff in our life that is out of whack, then we turn to Jesus, and he comes and does his healing Sabbath work.

We get tired in body and in *soul*. We need more than a twenty-four-hour armistice from work; we need an encounter with Jesus' healing power.

After all, the Sabbath is nothing more than a signpost, pointing forward, to the future . . .

Life after heaven

How you holding up?

You okay?

We're nearing the end, but there's one more thing we *have* to cover before we clock out. To prime you, this chapter is *key*, essential, vital, incredibly important. If we don't get this, the entire house of cards will fold to the ground.

Most of this book has been looking backward — to creation, the Garden, Adam, and how we got where we are. But honestly, most of the library that is the New Testament is looking *forward* — to the Garden-like city. It's not about where we've come from as much as where we're *going*. It's almost like the New Testament writers are leaning forward with a pneumatic hope, stretching their neck out to see what's just over the horizon.

All of which brings me to *this* book. This book has essentially been about work and rest and how they are central to our humanness.

But some questions have probably been nagging in the back of your head for a while now — *What does any of this have to do with eternity? Is there any connection between my work — my job or career in this life — and what I will experience in the next?*

After all, as the saying goes, "It's all going to burn."

Right?

If you think that way, you're not alone. The dominant view of the future, at least in the West, is that Jesus is going to come back, judge the world, and take us all away to heaven to live happily ever after.

This is essentially a theology of evacuation. The sentiment is, Let's get out of *here* and go somewhere *else*.

If this is true, if this is the hope of Jesus, then it raises the question, What's the point of work? Much less rest?

Why should we take our job or career or vocation or calling or art or music or justice or culture seriously if, in the end, it's all going into the cosmic trash can and we're going to a galaxy far, far away?

Doesn't it make more sense to just make enough money to live how we want, then get off work, go to church a lot, and give a little of our extra money to "spiritual" work, so we can get people into heaven when they die?

After all, that's what it's all about.

Right?

Not exactly.

That horrific phrase "It's all gonna burn" comes from a misreading of a letter written by Peter, one of Jesus' disciples. I would argue it's borderline heretical. Bare minimum, it's a warping of what Peter actually said. Listen to his statement:

"The day of the Lord will come like a thief. The heavens will disappear with a roar; the elements will be destroyed by fire, and the earth and everything done in it will be laid bare."[1]

There it is. In black and white. The heavens and the earth will be "destroyed."

Sounds pretty straightforward. Jesus comes back and it's worldwide Hiroshima. Game over. Cue the angel choir.

Yes, *except* that in context Peter is retelling the story of the flood, and in the paragraph right before this one he uses the exact same language. He says that in the flood, the earth was "destroyed" by water.

But we all know that story. The earth wasn't destroyed in the sense of wiped out or ceasing to exist; it was destroyed in that the slate was wiped clean. It was a global restart.

That's why Peter goes on to say the earth and all the work done in it will be "laid bare." In Greek it's the word *heurisko*, which means "exposed" or "seen for what it really is" or "discovered." Usually the word is translated "found."

So there is coming a day, when all the layers of smut and garbage and injustice and blood and exploitation will be burned up and the earth will be *found*, seen for what it *really* is, what God intended it to be all along.

Just as the earth was destroyed by water, it will be again, but this time by fire.

And in Peter's mind, this is a *good* thing.

His closing line is, "In keeping with his promise we are looking forward to a new heaven and a new earth, where righteousness dwells."[2]

So this isn't about the end of the time/space universe, but rather about its radical healing. The hope of Jesus isn't about somewhere *else*; it's about right here, on the planet he created and called good all those years ago.

And this could happen *at any minute*. "The day of the Lord will come like a thief" — a robber in the middle of the night. Peter is on pins and needles waiting for the day.

Now, the "day of the Lord" might sound like strange language to us, but this was standard, first-century Jewish verbiage. Jews like Peter and Jesus divided human history into two ages or periods of time — "this age" and "the age to come."

This age was marked by human sin and rebellion — violence, injustice, sickness, pain, suffering, the demonic, and, in the end, death.

But the age to come was marked by a return to Eden, a return to how it was supposed to be all along — peace, justice, flourishing, and life forever.

And in between this age and the age to come was the day of the Lord — a seam between the two epochs, a drastic, world-altering upheaval of the status quo.

The prophet Joel said, "The sun shall be turned into darkness, and the moon into blood, before the great and terrible day of the LORD come."[3] Now, don't take that literally. It's from a highly symbolic genre of literature called apocalyptic. That's a way of saying, it will be *earth shattering*. Everything will change.

But here's the best part — the age to come takes place *here*,
not somewhere else.

Listen to the prophet Isaiah's vision of the age to come:

> See, I will create
>   new heavens and a new earth.
> The former things will not be remembered,
>   nor will they come to mind.
> But be glad and rejoice forever
>   in what I will create,
> for I will create Jerusalem to be a delight
>   and its people a joy....
>
> They will *build houses* and dwell in them;
>   they will *plant vineyards* and eat their fruit ...
> my chosen ones will long enjoy
>   the *work* of their hands.
> They will not *labor in* vain,
>   nor will they bear children doomed to misfortune;
> for they will be a people blessed by the LORD.[4]

Notice all the language about working.

When Isaiah sees the future, he sees us building and farming
and eating and drinking and bursting with joy.

This is a far cry from how a lot of us think about the future.
Most people I know see the future in "heaven" as nothing

more than leisure. A combination eternal church service and eternal vacation. This is a reflection of American culture, not the Scriptures.

By now your image of Adam in the Garden shouldn't be of him sunbathing or lounging around in his bathrobe, but of him turning a forest into a city.

We were made to work, *and we will work forever.* And before you get sad about that, realize it's in a world where the curse has been undone. The "painful toil" is gone. We will not "labor in vain." Our work will be exciting, fun, challenging, rewarding, fascinating, energizing, significant, and custom fit for who we are.

And not just our work, but our rest as well.

Another prophecy about the age to come sounds like this,

> On this mountain the LORD Almighty will prepare
> a feast of rich food for all peoples,
> a banquet of aged wine —
> the best of meats and the finest of wines.[5]

So, the age to come is a *feast*, a party, a holiday with family and friends, from all over the world.

The prophet Joel goes so far as to say,

> In that day the mountains will drip new wine,
> and the hills will flow with milk.[6]

Oh man, that sounds good.

Amos sounds similar,

> "The days are coming," declares the LORD,
> "when the reaper will be overtaken by the plowman
> and the planter by the one treading grapes.
> New wine will drip from the mountains
> and flow from all the hills, . . .

> "They will rebuild the ruined cities and live in them.
> They will plant vineyards and drink their wine;
> they will make gardens and eat their fruit."[7]

Notice the seamless integration of work and rest, rebuilding and living in cities, planting and gardening, and eating and drinking, with no scarcity. Where the reaper can't even keep up with the plowman because there's so much abundance.

And we will live this way for a *very* long time.

Isaiah says it this way:

> On this mountain he will destroy
> the shroud that enfolds all peoples,
> the sheet that covers all nations;

he will swallow up death forever.[8]

Death will die and we will work and rest *forever.*

Sign

me

up.

Notice how earthy this poetry is. That's because the age to come takes place *here*, on Earth.

If this sounds strange to you, don't feel bad or stupid or out of the loop. You're not alone. Most people, at least in the late modern West, think of the future as a two-stage process:

Life, here on earth, in a body.

Followed by . . .

Life after death, in heaven or hell.

And this is a *glorious* hope for Jesus' followers. I'm watching my grandfather die right now. He was this strong, energetic, successful outdoorsman — runner, hiker, skier, explorer. But out of the blue he came down with a rare genetic lung disease, and his body, which he cared for *so well* all his years, is crumbling. Two years ago he was getting dropped off by a helicopter to ski down the Sierra Nevada mountains. Now he can't walk up the stairs. He's so out of breath he can barely whisper a sentence. It's excruciating to watch him in so much pain, *but* Grandpa Jack is at peace. Because he's a follower of Jesus. And to know that when he dies, he will live on in God's presence, is *so* comforting. I don't have to fear or worry or mourn as if it's goodbye forever, because this life is not all there is. There's more.

This hope is invaluable.

But it's also incomplete.

Contrary to how a lot of us think, the biblical authors write about the future as a *three-stage* process:

Life, here on earth, in a body.

Followed by ...

Life after death, in heaven or hades, with or without a body, it's unclear.

Followed by ...

Resurrection.

This, my friends, is where it gets interesting. Resurrection is what happens *after* heaven, when we come back here, in a body, on the earth, and we get on with the business of ruling the world. One scholar called it "Life *after* life after death."[9]

Now, in the Western church, we put the emphasis on stage two — heaven. But it might surprise you to learn that the New Testament says very little about life after death. In fact the common phrase "go to heaven when you die" is never even used in the Bible. Ever.

Most of the time it's just called "sleep" — a way of saying that the dead are still alive in a sense but are waiting for resurrection.

But then in two passages in Paul's writings, we read that at death we are "with the Lord" — so apparently, sleep is a metaphor. We are actually awake and aware of God's presence. But other than that, Paul doesn't say much, except that it will be a really good experience.[10]

The only in-depth passage about heaven in the New Testament is in *Revelation*. It's apocalyptic literature, so it's not clear what is symbolic and what is literal, but either way, the prophet John's vision of heaven is *very different* from how most of us think of it.

After painting a breathtaking vision of all heaven worshiping God on a throne at the center of the universe, he writes, "I saw under the altar the souls of those who had been slain because of the word of God and the testimony they had maintained.

They called out in a loud voice, 'How long, Sovereign Lord, holy and true, until you judge the inhabitants of the earth and avenge our blood?' Then each of them was given a white robe, and they were told to wait a little longer."[11]

This is a nuclear bomb on every popular book and movie about heaven that I know.

In *Revelation*, the dead are in heaven, waiting for resurrection, and in the meantime they are looking down at the injustice on earth, *grieving*, and crying out to God, "How long?!"

Until what?

Until God makes things right *on Earth*.

This is because, contrary to the popular saying, heaven is *not* our home. Earth is. Not Earth as it is now, but Earth as it will be in the future. Our hope isn't for another *place*, but another *time*. Yes, as followers of Jesus, we go to heaven when we die, but *we don't stay there*. If Jesus is a "ticket to heaven," as the preacher says, then he's a round-trip ticket, not a one-way. Because at the resurrection, we come *back*.

And this new world that we come back to is never once called heaven by *any* of the biblical authors.

Jesus called it "the renewal of all things."[12]

Paul called it "the kingdom of God" and "eternal life."[13]

Peter called it "the time ... for God to restore everything."[14]

Then later he reused the language of the prophet Isaiah and said, "In keeping with his promise we are looking forward to a new heaven and a new earth, where righteousness dwells."[15]

The writer John, picking up on Isaiah and his friend Peter said, "Then I saw 'a new heaven and a new earth.'"[16]

Pause for a second. A lot of people misread and misquote this line. It shows up three times in the Bible, so it's pretty important that we get it right.

First off, "heaven" here doesn't mean God's dwelling place; it just means the sky or the universe. This is a blatant echo to Genesis 1v1 — the first line in the Bible. "In the beginning God created the heavens and the earth." John is saying, in the future, God will *re-create* the heavens and the earth.

Secondly, the word "new" is *kainos* in Greek. It can be translated "renewed." Kind of like after you finish restoring an old, broken-down house or car or piece of furniture, and you say, "It's like *new*." That's the idea.

This isn't about God scrapping the earth and starting over; this is about God stripping it down to the studs, clearing out all the junk and grit and grime, and making it new again.

And in this new and renewed world, we won't be lounging around on a cloud with a loincloth on, singing "Amazing Grace" for millennia on end. Honestly, that sounds more like the *other* place . . .

Read *Revelation*! The last two chapters of the Bible are all about the future — what all of human history is building up to. And the story doesn't end with us going away to heaven, but rather, with heaven's invasion of Earth. We see Jesus and his followers who have died coming *back* from heaven to "rule over the earth."

The closing image isn't of a cloud or a harp or Raphael and his floating cupids; it's of a *city*. A city with walls and gates and streets and dwellings and a river and a forest and *culture*. As I said earlier, it's draped in language straight out of *Genesis*.

"A new heaven and a new earth."

"The tree of life."

"No longer will there be any curse."

"They will reign."

So it's not just a city . . .

It's a *Garden* city.

This is what's waiting for us. Not an eternal vacation in the sky, but an eternity of working and resting in *this world* completely remade from top to bottom by the Creator, ruling over *the earth,* side by side with Jesus himself, forever.

This is the hope of Jesus.

The people of the future

Let's take a step back, breathe it all in, and strip this down to the nuts and bolts.

All this talk about the future has MASSIVE implications for how we work and rest in the here and now.

You could put it this way: our eschatology shapes our ethics.[1]

Eschatology is a technical term used in theology; it's from the Greek word *eschaton*, meaning the end.

Eschatology. Theology of the end.

And how we view the end — the goal, the climax, what this

whole story is leading up to, *shapes* our ethics, how we *live* today.

It shapes what we do and don't do for a living.

What we value and what we don't care about.

What we do or don't spend money on.

How many hours we work each week. How often we rest, Sabbath, take a vacation.

If you think that you're en route to heaven — a place up in the sky, somewhere *else*, with no body, and a "spiritual" existence, then it's hard not to feel a sense of meaninglessness about your job or career or justice or cultural renewal in *this* world.

But if you read the Scriptures and wake up to the reality that your hope is grounded in *resurrection,* that you're on track for the age to come … Well, that changes everything, especially how you view work and rest.

Let's start with rest …

The Sabbath is a memorial, remember? A weekly reminder of two worlds — the one behind us *and* the one ahead of us. It's a signpost, pointing backward to the Garden and forward to the Garden city.

If this is true, it means that we don't have to get it all done *now*. We don't have to work ourselves into the ground, until we're scraping off the bone and there's nothing left.

But what about YOLO? I mean, you only live once.

Not if you're a follower of Jesus.

We have all eternity to live into God's world. We'll live another day, another week, another *millennium*. Yes, time is a precious commodity, but we're filthy rich. We have *plenty* of it.

So every Sabbath we can rest. Really, fully, honestly rest. The world's not going anywhere.

We make it our goal to acclimate and tune our body and our soul to the world we came from, to live at Eden's soothing pace. But we also make it our goal to anticipate and act out the coming world, to live as we will forever — eating, drinking, and *just enjoying* God's presence.

The Sabbath is a glimpse of the life that was and of the life that's coming.

Now, let's move on to work ...

The essence of following Jesus is using our work to cooperate with heaven's invasion of Earth.

I think of the end of 1 Corinthians 15 — the longest passage about resurrection and the age to come in the entire Bible. Fifty-eight verses of dense, heady, complex, in-depth, technical, charged, explosive eschatology. And listen to Paul's closing paragraph — this is the end of his sermon, his "practical application points":

"Therefore, my dear brothers and sisters, stand firm. Let nothing move you. Always give yourselves fully to the work of the Lord, because you know that your labor in the Lord is not in vain."[2]

So what Paul thinks resurrection means is that our "work" and "labor" are not in vain. They're not all for nothing. They *matter.*

Of course, we read "the work of the Lord" and "labor in the Lord" and *assume* Paul means evangelism or missionary work. But he doesn't say that. It's ambiguous and unclear and open to interpretation.

I bet that's on purpose.

What I'm getting at is all this eschatology, all this talk about the future, about resurrection and the age to come, should have a tectonic, pivotal, inspiring effect on our *work* in the here and now.

There's *so* much we could say about this, but here are four thoughts to land the book.

First off,

It needs to be said that good work is worthwhile *even if it's just for this age*, with no bearing on the age to come at all.

Whatever it is you do — cooking, building, teaching, writing, mothering, project managing, beehive keeping — if you do it as an act of worship to God and an expression of love and service to humanity, *that's enough*.

Work isn't a means to an end; it *is* an end.

I cannot emphasize this enough. Most people don't actually believe their work matters in the here and now. For its own sake. But it's incredibly true.

If all you do is fill a gas tank to get somebody on the road or set up a mortgage for somebody to buy a house or sell a jacket to keep somebody warm, that matters, all by itself. And it's enough.

Secondly,

Our work in this life is *practice* for our work in the coming life.

In one sense, what we do now matters, all by itself. We don't need to add anything onto it or spice it up. But in another sense, it's practice.

The philosopher Dallas Willard said this life is "training for reigning." As cheesy as that sounds, he's spot-on. Right now we are learning the skills we'll need forever in God's new world.

The Bible opens with God giving humans a vocation, a calling to rule, to look after his creation and make it flourish, and after a long, drawn-out detour through human history, the Bible ends with that vision finally coming to pass and even going *forward*.

Revelation — the last book in the Bible — is filled with royalty language ...

"(He) has made us to be a kingdom and priests."[3]

"I will give the right to sit with me on my throne."[4]

"They shall reign on the earth."[5]

"They ... will reign with him for a thousand years."[6]

"They will reign for ever and ever."[7]

So our future hope isn't *only* that Jesus will rule the universe. It is, but it's also that we'll rule right at his side. As Paul put it, "If we endure, *we will also reign with him*."[8]

God is looking for people he can rule the world with. Right now, we are *becoming* those kinds of people.

Learning how to fight laziness with hard work, and how to fight workaholism with Sabbath.

Learning how to handle money and sex and power.

Learning how to deal with technology and information in the digital age.

Learning how to live *over* the earth and not get crushed under its weight or fall prey to its seduction.

And I would argue that we're not just learning the skills of character, but we're learning the skills of the craft.

Isaiah and Amos were both pretty clear. We will "build houses" in the age to come. Theoretically, that means we'll need architects and contractors and electricians and plumbers and cabinet makers and furniture makers and interior designers and on down the list.

If you're an architect now and you love your work, you enjoy it, and you feel like you're good at it, who's to say you won't love it and do it forever?

If so, as you go to work each day and hone your skill, you're not just making a better world *now,* you're learning the skills, one day in the future, to make the *best* world.

Whoever you become will carry over into the next life. The

saying "You can't take it with you" may be true of stuff —
your car or that sweet new pair of shoes, but it's definitely
misleading. You will take the person you become with
you into God's future. And who you become is your most
valuable asset.

Not only that, but here's my third thought,

Some of the good work we do will actually last into God's
new world.

I really believe that.

In Revelation 14 we read that the dead "will rest from their
labor, for their deeds will follow them."[9]

Their deeds will follow them?

The word *deeds* is *ergon* in Greek. Usually it's translated
"work," but it can also be translated "occupation."

So our work will follow us? Maybe even our occupation will follow us, past death and into the age to come.

Later, in Revelation 21, we read about the Garden city, and
John writes "the kings of the earth will bring their splendor
into it.... The glory and honor of the nations will be brought
into it."[10]

This is an enigmatic statement at best, but it could mean that all good work, the accumulation of thousands of years of culture making, will somehow be brought into the made-new–Jerusalem.

Miroslav Volf, the brilliant Croatian philosopher/theologian from Yale, puts it this way:

"The noble products of human ingenuity, whatever is beautiful, true and good in human cultures, will be cleansed from impurity, perfected, and transfigured to become a part of God's new creation. They will form the 'building materials,' from which the glorified world will be made."[11]

To clarify, I'm not saying that if you're a textile designer and you weave a rug, that rug will be in the New Jerusalem. Not unless it is fireproof. The earth — and everything in it — *will be* "destroyed by fire."

But I *am* saying that when I envision the future, I imagine living in a home. My guess is it will have a rug or two. I imagine eating Thai food and drinking an almond milk latte and listening to Prelude from Suite No. 1 in G Major on a cello and riding a bicycle and flying in an airplane and reveling in all the good, beautiful, and true things that image bearers have come up with over the millennia of human history.

It's all the graffiti — the evil, ugly stuff that will disappear forever.

I think of chapter 3 in Paul's letter to the Corinthians. For me, it's a bit of a paradigm:

"Each one should *build* with care.... If anyone builds on this foundation using gold, silver, costly stones, wood, hay or straw, their *work* will be shown for what it is, because the Day will bring it to light. It will be revealed with fire, and the fire will test the *quality of each person's work*. If what has been built survives, the builder will receive a reward. If it is burned up, the builder will suffer loss but yet will be saved."[12]

This is Paul's take on the day of the Lord, and, just like Peter, he sees it as a day of fire, where all that is ugly will go away, and all that is beautiful and true will be shown for what it truly is.

Obviously, in context, this is a passage about church work, about building the people of God. And that may be all it's for. But my guess is you can broaden it out for *all* work.

There's a lot of human work that frankly will not survive the day of the Lord. It will not make it into God's new world.

Stuff like ...

War

Violence

Exploitation of the poor

Corrupt bureaucracy

Opulent waste

Damage to the environment

Gluttony

Drunkenness

Smut

R & B

(I'm just kidding on that last one. Kind of.)

All this stuff will be "burned up." And people who gave their life to "wood, hay or straw," the kind of work that is kindling for the fire, will have nothing to show for all their effort and energy. They'll make it "in," but barely. And with empty pockets.

But on the flip side, Paul's hope is that some human work *will* survive judgment and go on to find a place in the new creation. That somehow — and I have no idea how — all our work that is "gold, silver, costly stones," the kind of work that *matters*, will follow us into the age to come. God will find a way to take it, cleanse it, and integrate it into his new world.

New Testament scholar N. T. Wright said it this way:

"What you do in the present — by painting, preaching, singing, sewing, praying, teaching, building hospitals, digging wells, campaigning for justice, writing poems, caring for the needy, loving your neighbor as yourself — will last into God's future. These activities are not simply ways of making the present life a little less beastly, a little more bearable, until the day when we leave it behind altogether (as the hymn so mistakenly puts it). They are part of what we may call building for God's kingdom."[13]

I love that language: building *for* God's kingdom. We can't build the kingdom, only Jesus can do that. But we can build *for* the kingdom. We can make bricks, and God, the master builder, can find a way to enfold them into his masterpiece.

So, for my architect friend Tony, the houses he makes in this life won't last forever, but we'll need houses in the coming world. And every single design, every idea, every innovation, every new green, sustainable technology he comes up with has the potential to follow him into the age to come.

If that doesn't make you want to get really good at your job, I have no clue what will.

Then, lastly,

Know that all good work done in this age will be rewarded in the age to come.

There is far more continuity between this age and the age to come than most of us think. There is a direct correlation between how we live now and how we will live forever. Or to be more precise, between *how* we rule now and how *much* we will rule over forever.

A good chunk of Jesus' parables were about work — commerce, trade, money, management, employer-employee relationships, and so on. A lot of them end by basically saying that how you work now has a direct effect on how you will work in the future.

I think of the parable in Luke 19 about the "man of noble birth" (read, king) who went on a long journey. Before he left, he gave each of his servants a mina — a large sum of money. When he came back, he wanted an accounting for his investment.

The first servant comes up and says, "Sir, your mina has earned five more."

And what does the king say?

"You take charge of *five* cities."[14]

Five minas, five cities.

Responsibility now, more responsibility later.

So there is a *one-to-one* reciprocity between how we work now and the kind of work we will do forever.

Of course, we read this and *assume* that "take charge of five cities" is a metaphor, and it probably is. But isn't this what Adam was supposed to do all along? Rule? Take a garden and make a city?

What if it's *not* a metaphor?

Either way, the point still stands: the reward for work well-done in this age isn't a mansion and a Maserati in heaven, as if the best God can do is acquiesce to capitalism's perversion of the American dream; it's *more* work and *more* responsibility in God's new world.

And that should excite you! Curse-free, exhilarating, satisfying work. And *responsibility*, a sense that what you do is important in the grand scheme of things.

Even if your work now doesn't feel that way. Even if you're a sanitation engineer or a gofer on a construction crew or housekeeping for a hotel or a checker at Whole Foods. Maybe you love what you do, maybe you hate it. Maybe you can change what you do, maybe you're stuck. But either way, you can do it for a reward.

I absolutely love what Paul writes to the slaves in Colossae:

"Whatever you do, work at it with all your heart, as working for the Lord, not for human masters, since you know that you will receive an inheritance from the Lord as a reward. It is the Lord Christ you are serving."[15]

Now, Paul's not condoning slavery here. Even if he was, slavery in the ancient Mediterranean was totally different than the African American slave trade, or the human trafficking going on in India or Southeast Asia right now. It wasn't based on ethnicity, and it usually wasn't for life. It was closer to how I imagine the life of an illegal immigrant working on a farm somewhere in California or Texas.

Still, can you think of a worse job? It was probably filled with the mundane — cleaning the floor, washing the dishes, weeding around the house, working in the field — with no control over what you do or don't do every day.

And it's to *slaves* that Paul writes *whatever you do*, give it your very best because you're actually not working for your human master; you're working for Jesus himself.

And ...

"You will receive an inheritance."

Meaning ...

God will reward you *for all work done in his name*. Even if it's not sexy or glamorous or hip or prestigious. Even if your work isn't rescuing girls out of the sex trade, or writing music, or teaching at an Ivy League school, or filmmaking — the kind of culture-making work we fantasize about. Even if your work is washing dirty dishes in the back room of a cheap restaurant, it will be rewarded as long as it's done for Jesus. Not just to get a paycheck by doing the bare minimum until the end of your shift, but as an act of worship and service to God and humanity.

Because if you're faithful with your one mina now, then in the world to come, you will *rule*. You will finally get to do the kind of work you love. In the meantime, don't give up. Don't give in. You're headed for an "inheritance."

So, to end (and I really mean it this time) . . .

I just read this great story about the French composer Olivier Messiaen and his famous piece *Quartet for the End of Time*. It was written in the winter of 1941. Messiaen was captured by the Nazis and put in Stalag 8-A, a concentration camp in Görlitz, Germany. While in prison, facing a brutally cruel lifestyle, he spent time reading the four gospels and *Revelation*. As a follower of Jesus, he was somehow filled with hope for the world, right in the middle of hell on Earth. When he realized there were three other famous musicians in the camp, he found four instruments — a cello with a missing string, a beat up violin, a well-worn clarinet, and a piano with keys that stuck together — and he composed an incredible piece of chamber music. The *New Yorker* later called it "the most ethereally beautiful music of the twentieth century."[16] They first played it in January, right in the middle of the concentration camp, to hundreds of prisoners *and guards*, in the freezing cold. Messiaen later said, "The cold was excruciating, the Stalag buried under snow, the four performers played on broken down instruments ... but never have I had an audience who listened with such rapt attention."[17]

I tell you this story because I can't think of a more dramatic or more fitting picture of the kind of work we are to do on this side of resurrection.

We are the people of the future *in the present*.

Paul said, "If anyone is in Christ, he is a new creation."[18]

So, new creation is here *now*; it's bursting out through the cracks in the pavement, and it's starting with *us*.

We're the vanguard, the advance sign of what's coming for the whole world.

So we work in the *present* world — right in the middle of all the chaos and entropy and suffering and pain — for a glimpse of the *future* world, set free from evil and death itself.

And the hope is that as we do whatever it is we do, people

will see our work, and, shivering in the cold, will come a little closer, listen to the music, and maybe, just maybe, start to see that in the middle of all the sorrow and emptiness and trauma of this life, something new is brewing, seeping up through the ground, breaking in.

Or as a teacher I follow once said, "The kingdom of heaven is at hand."

Epilogue: Re-defining greatness

We are born with a desire to be great.

We come out of the womb screaming for a life of meaning and purpose and, well, significance. We want to leave the world better off than we found it. To somehow have our name live on long after we've stopped breathing.

We grow up dreaming of a life that's a story worth telling.

Ask a child — a four- or five-year-old — What do you want to be when you grow up? None of them say, "I want to be an accountant" or "I'm thinking insurance" or "I feel a pull to tax law."

If they did, we would get them into therapy. Fast.

No, they say stuff like astronaut or police officer or ballerina. Ninja is a popular choice in my house, as is rock star and Jedi Knight.

My point is that as *children* we have a desire to do something that matters.

Put simply, we want to be great.

Nobody just wants to be a carbon footprint and take up space. Nobody just wants to go through life, work a job, buy a house, pay taxes, amass stuff, and then retire with a condo in Florida and a Comcast subscription.

Most of us want *more* out of the short breath that is our existence.

Now, over the years, we might ignore this desire or suppress it or deny it or lock it in the basement and starve it to death, but it's unshakable. It won't go away. No matter how hard we try to stomp it out, it's *there*, from our first breath.

Think of the mythology of American culture.

You're thinking, *We have mythology?*

Of course.

The Greeks had Zeus and Hercules and Poseidon; we have Batman and Superman and the Avengers. The ancient world had Homer's *Iliad*; we have DC Comics.

And superheroes are basically the same thing to a tee:

Human beings,

with special powers,

who serve the weak,

and save the world.

It's the same formulaic story over and over again. And we eat it up. At this rate, I'll live to see *The Avengers 7.*

Why is that? I think it's because mythology taps into our humanness. The first human was a king. Even if we're born into abject poverty, there's royalty in our blood. We were made to rule the world. The pull to greatness is in our DNA.

In fact, I would argue the desire to be great was put there by the Creator himself. After all, we're made in his image.

The problem is this desire, which in its embryonic, innocent state is so, so right, is quickly warped and soiled and bent out of shape by the ego.

We devolve from a desire to be great to a desire to be *thought of* as great.

From a desire to serve the weak to a desire to be served *by* the weak.

From a desire to save the world to a desire to *have* it.

The cultural iconoclast Madonna said it best in her biography:

"I have an iron will, and all of my will has always been to conquer some horrible feeling of inadequacy.... I push past one spell of it and discover myself as a special human being, and then I get to another stage and think I'm mediocre and uninteresting.... Again and again. My drive in life is from this horrible fear of being mediocre. And that's always pushing me, pushing me. Because even though I've become Somebody, I still have to prove I'm Somebody. My struggle has never ended and it probably never will."[1]

She does such a great job of capturing the zeitgeist of our generation. We were born into wealth. And with wealth comes the freedom to dream. If I had a dollar for every person who said, "I'm a dreamer," well, I could at least eat out more often. And this isn't a bad thing, at all.

But so many of us dream the wrong kind of dreams. Flat, one-dimensional, anemic dreams where the story is all about us. Where we're the hero.

Everybody wants to be spectacular.

The question is, How do we live in this tension? Between our childlike dreams to be and do something that matters, and our more adult, ugly desires for power and control and fame and celebrity status, another house, another vacation, another leg up on the world? How do we hang on to the right desires — even into adulthood — but at the same time, eject all the others?

This question isn't new. Followers of Jesus have been asking it for a very long time.

One of my favorite stories in the Gospels is where the disciples are fighting over "who was the greatest."[2] Can you imagine that conversation?

"I should be first, I'm the oldest."

"No, you couldn't even walk on water for five minutes!"

"Well, at least I tried. You just sat in the boat."

"Hey, come on, everybody knows I'm his favorite disciple. I'm even thinking of writing a memoir."

And then all of the sudden you turn around and there's your rabbi, Jesus, staring at you with that same gentle-but-annoyed look on his face.

Awkward ...

But Jesus' response isn't what I would expect:

"Sitting down, Jesus called the Twelve and said, 'Anyone who wants to be first must be the very last, and the servant of all.'"

Notice that Jesus doesn't castigate the disciples for their desire to be great. I would expect him to go off on Peter and the rest, but he doesn't. Instead, he *redefines* greatness.

The word "first" can also be translated "great." Jesus essentially says, "You desire to be great? Okay, I put that in you. Here's how — become a servant."

The word "servant" is *diakanos*. It means "one who waits on tables." It can even be translated "waiter," like at a restaurant.

What a fascinating example of greatness. He could have said, Be like a king, a warrior, a revolutionary, a poet, an artist — anything. But instead he chose servant.

The striking thing about a servant is that they exist to make *others'* lives better. If we're honest, most of us live the other way around, myself included. But to Jesus, the word *great* is synonymous with the word *servant*.

This was unheard of in Jesus' day. It was a stratified society — even more than ours today.

Jews and gentiles.

Male and female.

Citizens and noncitizens.

Rich and poor.

Masters and servants.

And servants were at the very bottom of the social ladder. It was a demeaning, dishonorable role.

At one point the Greek philosopher Plato said, "How can a man be happy when he has to serve someone?"[3] He was summing up the ethos of the day. But to Jesus, the way to happiness, to the "life that is truly life," was *through* serving other people.[4]

Have you ever noticed that people who are self-focused and narcissistic are usually really unhappy, if not depressed? Sadly, I know this from experience. But have you also noticed that people who are generally others-focused and more selfless are usually very happy? That's not a coincidence. It's the way of Jesus in action. When we're down, one of the best things we can do is serve somebody *else*. It's the backdoor to joy. And it's always unlocked.

But nobody thought this way in the ancient world. Even today, not much has changed. Most of us want to be great so that other people will serve *us*. Jesus is calling us out. He's saying that greatness is when we love and serve *others*.

After all, the world itself was born out of the womb of God's love. He just had too much of it to keep it all inside. It ended up spilling out. And God made the world, not to get something *from* us, but rather as a gift *for* us to enjoy and play in and make something of.

In the same way, when we live and work, not to get what we can from others, but rather to love and serve them, we're harmonizing with the heart of God himself. And one of the best possible ways we can love and serve people is to show up for work every day. And to do our work, not to get ahead, or make more money, or become famous, but to love and serve God and neighbor. And when we do that, we start to reclaim our humanness.

This is what Jesus is getting at with his disciples. To make his point, Jesus followed up his teaching with a prop:

"He took a little child whom he placed among them. Taking the child in his arms, he said to them, 'Whoever welcomes one of these little children in my name welcomes me; and whoever welcomes me does not welcome me but the one who sent me."[5]

So what does greatness look like in real life?

A little kid on Jesus' lap.

Now, keep in mind, this is first-century Galilee. It wasn't like today. We live in what one journalist called a "Kindergarchy" — a nation under the rule of children.[6] Most of the time, children get whatever the heck they want. Plus, we romanticize children as an example of wonder and innocence and courage.

None of that was true in Jesus' day. Children were loved by mom and dad, sure, but they were at the bottom of the social pile — right next to servants.

Then Jesus comes along and says that greatness is found in serving others, in fact, in serving *children* — people who are unimportant and don't have any status. People on the margin of society.

That's greatness.

Of course, the disciples are oblivious to Jesus' teaching. They don't get it. In the *next line*, we read, " 'Teacher,' said John, 'we saw someone driving out demons in your name and we told him to stop, because he was not one of us.' "

So they see some guy driving out demons — which I think we could all agree is a *good* thing? — and they're jealous, insecure, posturing, and manipulative. Trying to shut his little exorcism start-up down.

Ironically, the story *right* before this one is about how the disciples were supposed to cast out a demon, but they couldn't do it.

Ouch.

The root of this is what the writers of the Bible call envy. Envy is when you covet another person's story. What greed is to money, envy is to life as a whole. It's when you look at a coworker or sibling or friend from college or celebrity and think, *I want that life.*

So we elbow-throw and work overtime and stress out and maybe even lie and cheat and fight tooth and nail to get ahead of the pack, but it's a vicious cycle because no matter how smart or educated or gifted or successful or wealthy or famous or beautiful you are, *there will always be somebody* who is smarter, better educated, more gifted, more successful, wealthier, or who has more Twitter followers or flatter abs. Hopefully not both.

There will always be somebody better than you.

Even if you manage to climb to the top of the pile, life then becomes an endless game of King of the Hill, and it's only a matter of time until you're knocked down by some young gun coming up behind you.

That's why so many of us live with ennui and angst and a mild resentment at the world, or at least a little bit of disillusionment. No matter what we do, it never feels like it's *enough*.

Seriously, my agenda here isn't to bum you out or discourage you from chasing after your dreams — it's just to state the obvious: you will always live in somebody's shadow. Always.

That's why envy sucks the joy right out of life. Because rather than enjoying who you are and what you do and the life that's spread out in front of you, you covet somebody else's story.

"I wish I was married like Sarah."

"I wish I was as beautiful as Joy."

"I wish I had Tom's job."

"I wish I was as successful as Jack."

And no matter who we become or how much we achieve, there's always *someone* out there who makes us oh-so-aware of our inadequacy.

"We saw someone driving out demons in your name and we told him to stop."

That line, by the way, is *right after* Jesus' teaching on greatness. When you read the story in Mark, the transition is abrupt and clunky. One minute Jesus is teaching on greatness with a child in his lap, and two seconds later the disciples are ratting out some dude for casting out demons.

Huh?

It's the writer's way of saying, *they don't get it.*

It would be easy to crack a joke here — to mock or ridicule the disciples for such blatant stupidity. But how often are we *just* as oblivious and dull? How often do we read Jesus' teachings about suffering and self-sacrifice, nod our head, and say, "Yes. Right. Mhhm," and then go right on self-promoting and gossiping and posturing and arguing about who is the greatest.

Thankfully, once again, Jesus doesn't lay into his guys. He goes on to say, "Don't stop him ... for whoever is not against us is for us."

Shocking. Jesus doesn't want the guy to stop driving out demons in order to pacify his disciples' egos.

Then he says this, "Truly I tell you, anyone who gives you a cup of water in my name because you belong to the Messiah will certainly not lose their reward."

So apparently, there's a reward, with our name on it. God's just waiting for us to do something reward-worthy.

And what is Jesus' example of work deserving of a reward from God himself?

A glass of water.

A small, insignificant, nonglamourous act of love and service.

It's easy to think that to be great and to get a reward from God, we have to do something high status. We have to change the world. Something Ted-Talk, Nobel-Peace-Prize quality.

And hopefully, God will reward that kind of stuff. But Jesus makes it clear that he'll also reward the stuff nobody knows about. The hard, mundane, thankless work of mothers and mechanics and second-grade teachers and garbage-truck drivers and the woman who does your dry cleaning. Work that doesn't get much attention or applause.

Honestly, sometimes I wonder if the high-status stuff will go *un*rewarded, because it's so easy to do the right thing for all the wrong reasons — for money or hubris or to prove your father wrong or become famous.

Maybe that's just me. But I don't think so.

"The day of the LORD," as the biblical writers call it, will be the great reversal. The upending of the status quo. The rich and famous might just fade into obscurity, and the unknown and humble and shy might just stand at the front of the line if you can get them to.

You never know, the first could even end up last, and the last, first. I feel like I've heard that somewhere.

So, to end …

I wrote this book to flood the engine of your dreams with nitrogen. I hope and pray that reading this gives you a shot of vision and courage and faith to step out and do whatever it is that God had in mind the day he thought you up.

Go to school. Get your PhD.

Drop out of school. Start a business.

Become a surgeon or a professional luchador.

Move to the inner city and work for justice in the middle of gentrification. Or move to Tribeka, make a billion dollars, and give it all away to the kingdom.

Invest in your children like every day is your last. Treat them like the future world-makers they actually are.

Solve the energy crisis.

Will somebody *please* come up with an alternative to the ketchup packet??

If you could do *anything* ...

You're a king, a queen. So rule the world.

Chase the sun over the horizon and drag the rest of us with you. I'm behind you all the way.

Just remember one last thing: if your dreams are all about you, *then your dreams are way too small.* You need to dream larger. Larger than your job or career or net worth or name or body. You need dreams as large as Jesus' vision of the kingdom.

A kingdom where greatness has been radically redefined around a crucified Messiah. Where children are the guests of honor. Where servants lead and leaders serve. Where the last are first.

Whatever your calling is, whatever you end up doing with your life — please, *please* don't do it for yourself. That's such an overdone, cliché, uncreative way of living. We've been there, done that. It's a waste of oxygen.

Do your work as an expression of love and service, ultimately to God, and then to your neighbor.

Maybe you'll make a ton of money, or maybe you'll just have enough.

Maybe you'll become a household name all over the world. The odds are, you won't.

Maybe you'll see your reward this side of resurrection, or maybe not until the next.

But none of that matters. That's not why you do it. You do it because God *made* you to do it. Because it's good. Because it has a bearing on this world and the world to come. Because when all is said and done, it *matters.*

So to anybody reading this book, wherever you are, whatever you do — may you become *great,* in the full, deep, true, panoramic sense of the word.

One glass of water at a time.

And I heard a loud voice from the throne saying, "Look! God's dwelling place is now among the people, and he will dwell with them. They will be his people, and God himself will be with them and be their God." ... One of the seven angels who had

the seven bowls full of
the seven last plagues
came and said to me,
"Come, I will show you
the bride, the wife of
the Lamb." And he
carried me away in
the Spirit to a moun-
tain great and high,
and showed me the
Holy City, Jerusalem,
coming down out of

heaven from God. It shone with the glory of God, and its brilliance was like that of a very precious jewel, like a jasper, clear as crystal. It had a great, high wall with twelve gates, and with twelve angels at the gates. On the gates were written the names of the twelve tribes of Israel. There were three gates on the east, three on the north, three on the south and three on the west. The wall of the city had twelve foundations, and on them were the names of the twelve apostles of the Lamb. The angel who talked with me

had a measuring rod
of gold to measure
the city, its gates and
its walls. The city was
laid out like a square,
as long as it was wide.
He measured the city
with the rod and found
it to be 12,000 stadia
in length, and as wide
and high as it is long.
The angel measured

the wall using human measurement, and it was 144 cubits thick. The wall was made of jasper, and the city of pure gold, as pure as glass. The foundations of the city walls were decorated with every kind of precious stone. The first foundation was jasper, the second sapphire, the third agate, the fourth emerald, the fifth onyx, the sixth ruby, the seventh chrysolite, the eighth beryl, the ninth topaz, the tenth turquoise, the eleventh jacinth, and the twelfth amethyst. The twelve gates were twelve pearls, each gate made of a single pearl. The great street of the city was of gold, as pure as transparent glass. I did not see a temple in the city, because the Lord God Almighty and the Lamb are its temple. The city does not need the sun or the moon to shine on it, for the glory of God gives it light, and the Lamb is its lamp. The nations will walk by its light, and the kings of the earth will bring their splendor into it. On no day will its gates ever be shut, for there will be no night there. The glory and honor of the nations will be brought into it. Nothing impure will ever enter it, nor will anyone who does what is shameful or deceitful, but only those whose names are written in the Lamb's book of life. Then the angel showed me the river of the water of life, as clear as crystal, flowing from the throne of

God and of the Lamb
down the middle of
the great street of the
city. On each side of
the river stood the tree
of life, bearing twelve
crops of fruit, yielding
its fruit every month.
And the leaves of the
tree are for the heal-
ing of the nations. No
longer will there be any

curse. The throne of God and of the Lamb will be in the city, and his servants will serve him. They will see his face, and his name will be on their fore-heads. There will be no more night. They will not need the light of a lamp or the light of the sun, for the Lord God

will give them light.
And they will reign for
ever and ever.

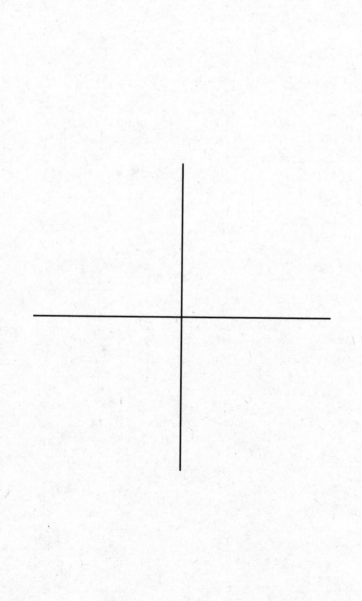

Notes

Welcome to the art of being human

1. Take that, San Francisco and Melbourne.
2. The odds are I can't sit down for a cup of coffee with you unless you live in my city, but my first book is all about this, and basically all I have to say is in there. It's called *My Name is Hope: Anxiety, Depression, and Life after Melancholy* (Portland: Graphe Publishing, 2011). You can get it on Amazon.com.
3. That said, a growing number of doctors and psychiatrists are changing how they think to a far more holistic view. For a dizzying (and terrifying) read on the controversy, pick up Robert Whitaker's Anatomy of an Epidemic: Magic Bullets, Psychi-atric Drugs and the Astonishing Rise of Mental Illness (New York: Random House, 2010).
4. This is an example of sar-casm. It will not be the last in this book.
5. Forgive me for degenerat-ing into the stereotypes we all hate. But I think this one's basically true.
6. This line is a steal from Tom Nelson's fabulous book *Work Matters: Connecting Sunday Worship to Monday Work* (Whea-ton, IL: Crossway, 2011), 15.
7. 1/24th, to be exact, not count-ing the days I oversleep, which never happens …
8. If you want to get technical, here's a quote from a top-shelf scholar, J. Richard Middleton: "A Hebrew jussive with uncon-verted *wāw* (*wĕyirdû*, and let

them rule) that follows a cohortative (*naʿăśeh*, let us make) always expresses the intention or aim of the first-person perspective (singular or plural) represented by the cohortative. The syntax, in other words, points to 'rule' as the *purpose*, not simply the consequence or result of the *imago Dei*." *The Liberating Image: The* Imago Dei *in Genesis 1* (Grand Rapids: Brazos, 2005), 53.

Kings and queens

1. Genesis 1v1.
2. This is in the next verse, Genesis 1v2.
3. Genesis 1v31.
4. This is actually Genesis 2v2, but it's the end of the first story in the Bible.
5. Although, sadly, that's how a lot of Americans read them.
6. This is way above my pay grade, but I like the theory of Pentateuchal scholar John Sailhammer. Basically, his take

is that Moses was kind of like a documentary filmmaker. He put together all sorts of sources — oral and written — into a cohesive story and then added all his own stuff. Then late, probably around the time of the exile, or even after it, an editor went through and updated it for the cannon. People like to think of Ezra as the editor, but we have no way of knowing. This theory makes the most sense to me. To learn more, read John Sailhammer's *The Meaning of the Pentateuch: Revelation, Composition and Interpretation* (Downers Grove, IL: InterVarsity, 2009). Incredible scholarship.
7. The best book I've read on all this is Richard Middleton's *Liberating Image*. It's a bit thick, but the best thing I've read on the image of God.
8. Genesis 1v26–27.
9. Re was also the national deity of Egypt. Also, the name *Rameses* — popular in literature and

films about Pharaoh — means "Re is the one who begot him."

10. Again, see J. Richard Middleton's *Liberating Image*.

11. Technically, we *think* this is where we get that saying. We're not really sure. Either way, my point still stands. Here's an interesting article on it: Jonathan K. Crane, "Put the Kibosh on It: Ethics Scholar Reflects on Language and Environmental Consequences," *Emory University Center for Ethics* (September 23, 2011), http://emoryethics.blogspot.com/2011/09/put-kibosh-on-it-ethics-scholar.html.

12. Genesis 4v17.

13. Genesis 4v20–21.

14. Also Genesis 4v20.

15. Genesis 9v20.

16. Genesis 9v21.

17. Genesis 19v30–38.

18. Genesis 4v23.

19. Genesis 4v1–20.

20. Exodus 3, Exodus 19, and 1 Kings 19.

21. 1 Corinthians 15v21, 45.

22. This is Romans 5v14 in N. T. Wright's translation from *The Kingdom New Testament: A Contemporary Translation* (New York: HarperCollins, 2011).

23. Romans 5v17.

24. Thanks to N. T. Wright for teaching me this, and about a billion other things. Seriously, his book *After You Believe: Why Christian Character Matters* (New York: HarperCollins, 2010) has some great stuff in it based on this idea.

25. The first theologian to notice what Paul was up to here was the early church father Irenaeus, writing just a few years after the New Testament. He grew up in Paul's church and had 20/20 vision on what Paul was getting at. He called this "recapitulation theory of atonement." That's a fancy way of saying that what God was doing through the Messiah's death and resurrection was a "recapitulation" or a summary of what Adam was supposed to do all along — reign, or rule. It's a grossly underemphasized facet of the atonement.

26. Revelation 1v5 and 19v16.

27. Mark 16v19.

28. It's easy for all the talk in the church about how we're saved by faith, *not* by works, to lead to a negative, warped view of work in general. And while it's true that we're saved by Jesus' work and not our own, that's just the beginning. From there we "work out our salvation with fear and trembling." We enflesh Jesus' way.

A place called Delight

1. Genesis 1v27.

2. Genesis 1v28.

3. Dr. Tim Mackie, the legend. The only professor I know who rides a skateboard to work.

4. All of this has been from Genesis 2v5, 7, 8, 15.

5. To clarify, it's not the *only* word used for "worship" in the Hebrew Bible. In my Bible, the NIV, *abad* is translated as "worship" 52 out of 285 times.

6. Genesis 2v9–15, emphasis added.

7. This is from Tim Keller's *Every Good Endeavor: Connecting Your Work to God's Work* (London: Hodder & Stoughton, 2012), 59, and it inspired this entire section. Thanks to Keller for being Keller.

8. This entire page is my reworking of Tim Keller's definition of work. It's one of my favorite parts in his brilliant book.

9. I was first exposed to this way of thinking in N. T. Wright's *After You Believe: Why Christian Character Matters* (New York: HarperCollins, 2010).

10. And that's just in the first paragraph of Revelation 22.

11. 1 Corinthians 3v6.

12. This is 1 Corinthians 3v9 from the *Holman Christian Standard Bible*. Each translation is a little bit different.

The unearthing of a calling

1. Okay, this is super cool. You can go to https://www.census.gov/popclock/, and they have a second-by-second update on world population. Do it. It's fun.
2. I'm drinking Stumptown today.
3. John 10v10 WE.
4. A ton of this section was inspired by Parker J. Palmer, *Let Your Life Speak: Listening for the Voice of Vocation* (San Francisco: Jossey-Bass, 1999). Incredible work.
5. 1 Thessalonians 4v11.
6. From Frederick Buechner, *Wishful Thinking: A Theological ABC* (New York: Harper & Row, 1973), 95.
7. This is from Luke 6v27–28. It's also in Matthew's Sermon on the Mount. Obviously, this is a complex, emotional, divisive subject that followers of Jesus don't all agree on. For a fantastic overview of the Bible's teaching on violence, read *Fight: A Christian Case for Non-Violence* by Preston Sprinkle (Colorado Springs: David C. Cook, 2013). I can't recommend it enough.
8. This way of thinking is called "meticulous providence" in theology. Sometimes it goes by the shorthand "God's sovereignty." Usually it's found in hyper-Calvinism. I very much disagree.
9. Proverbs 11v14 ESV.
10. Palmer, *Let Your Life Speak*, 7–8. So, so, sooo good. It inspired a *ton* of this chapter.

Everything is spiritual

1. That was my mandatory *Princess Bride* quote.
2. The word *pnuematikos*, or "spiritual," does show up in the New Testament, mostly in the writings of Paul. But it's not used how most of us use it. Most people think *spiritual* means esoteric, immaterial, otherworldly, enigmatic or deep, mystic experiences with God. But in Paul's theology it

means "animated by the Spirit of God." It's from the root word *pneuma*, where we get the word *pneumatic*. It's this driving, empowering presence in us to do what we're called to do — *on Earth*. It has nothing to do with material/immaterial. That's why in 1 Corinthians 2 he puts all humans into two categories. The "spiritual" are all followers of Jesus who have his Spirit; everybody else is *not* spiritual. Fascinating.

3. This language comes from the *Everything Is Spiritual* tour DVD by Rob Bell (Grand Rapids: Zondervan, 2007).

4. Although, tragically, this is still how a lot of American Christians think. *Please* read N. T. Wright's *Surprised by Hope: Rethinking Heaven, the Resurrection, and the Mission of the Church* (San Francisco: HarperOne, 2008) if you want to wrap your head around what Jesus and the biblical authors have to say about the future of God's world.

5. For a great read on what the kingdom of God is (and isn't), pick up Scot McKnight's *Kingdom Conspiracy: Returning to the Radical Mission of the Local Church* (Grand Rapids: Brazos, 2014). Paradigm changing work.

6. 1 Peter 2v9.

7. By the way, I in *no* way mean this as an anti-Catholic bash. I have some very good friends who are Catholic. This is a chapter about work, not an oversimplification of Catholicism. Still, I disagree on the whole priests bit …

8. The same Greek word — *diakonos* — is translated "ministry," "service," and "deacon" in the NIV.

9. Rob Bell, *Velvet Elvis: Repainting the Christian Faith* (San Francisco: HarperOne, 2012), 80.

10. 1 Thessalonians 2v9. In context, it's about tent making.

Kavod

1. Matt Eastvold: http://eastvold
furniture.com/.
2. 2 Chronicles 7v1–3,
emphasis added.
3. Psalm 19v1.
4. Habakkuk 2v14.
5. 1 Corinthians 10v31.
6. This is a great phrase used in
theology for the now and not-
yet-ness of the kingdom of God.
I think George Ladd was the first
to coin this phrase in his book
*The Presence of the Future: The
Eschatology of Biblical Real-
ism* (Grand Rapids: Eerdmans,
1996).
7. I put this in quotes not to
downplay the role of a missionary, but to recognize what a
fuzzy word it is. Technically, *all*
followers of Jesus are "sent-
ones" or "missionaries."
8. Check out Stephen's latest
work at www.stephenkenn.com.
9. John R. W. Stott, *Issues
Facing Christians Today* (Grand
Rapids: Zondervan, 2006), 225.

10. Romans 1v20.
11. Psalm 19v1; this is
my paraphrase.
12. Genesis 2v9.
13. Exodus 31v2–5, emphasis
added; God is the one speaking
in this verse.
14. This is from Witherington's book *Work: A Kingdom
Perspective on Labor* (Grand
Rapids: Eerdmans, 2011), 51. It's
really good.
15. 1 Thessalonians 4v11–12.
16. 2 Corinthians 3v18.
17. Irenaeus, *Against Heresies*
Book 4, 20:5–7.
18. 1,126 to be exact.

Kazam! Machine

1. We think. We don't actually know. About Ben that is.
But it definitely is a misquote
of somebody!
2. His name is Ryan Devens,
and he just started a new
company. Check it out at
www.tailorskeep.com.
3. This entire paragraph was

inspired by Dallas Willard. His book *The Divine Conspiracy* (San Francisco: HarperSan-Francisco, 1998) is one of my top-three favorite books of all time. His vision of discipleship is essential. Dallas, you are missed. See you at the resurrection.

4. This story is in Mark 1v9–11.

5. See Psalm 2.

6. This is the writer Mark's summary of Jesus' gospel, in Mark 1v14–15.

7. Mark 1v38, emphasis added.

8. Mark 1v39.

9. He also uses the word *thaumazo*.

10. Mark 7v37.

11. Luke 9v51 ESV.

12. Now we're in John 17v4.

13. John 19v30, emphasis added.

14. I'm referring to Dale S. Kuehne. His book *Sex and the iWorld: Rethinking Relationships beyond an Age of Individualism* (Grand Rapids: Baker, 2009) is fantastic.

15. John 1v19–23, emphasis added.

16. From Martin Buber, *Tales of the Hasidim* (New York: Schocken, 1991), 251.

17. The French writer Voltaire originally said this.

18. Proverbs 22v29.

19. Dorothy L. Sayers, "Why Work?" *Creed or Chaos? And Other Essays in Popular Theology* (Manchester: Sophia Institute, 1995), 106.

20. Romans 12v6. In Ephesians 4v7 he says something similar: "To each one of us grace has been given as Christ apportioned it."

21. Mike Erre, that is. Download his podcasts here: evfreefullerton.com.

22. This is from Frank's self-published book, *The Shape of Design* (2012), but you can watch a short video with the story here: http://frankchimero .com/talks/the-long-hard-stupid -way/transcript/.

23. What we call a "missional community."

24. I first read this in *Outliers: The Story of Success* (Boston: Little, Brown, 2007), my favorite book by Malcolm Gladwell.

25. The award was from *Time* magazine. If you want to see a picture of the chair, go to http://www.dwr.com/product/eames-molded-plywood-lounge-chair-lcw.do. I'm sure you'll recognize it. Sadly, it's no longer made with bicycles pumps.

Cursed is the ground

1. Genesis 1v28 *again*.

2. *Eden* is a Hebrew word meaning "delight."

3. Genesis 3v16.

4. Genesis 3v17 – 18.

5. Thomas David Wheeler, "Silicon Valley to Millennials: Drop Dead," *CNN.com* (March 18, 2015), http://www.cnn.com/2015/03/18/opinions/wheeler-silicon-valley-jobs/.

6. "70% of US Workers Are Not Engaged at Work," report *State of the American Workplace*, Gallup.com, http://www.gallup.com/services/178514/state-american-workplace.aspx

7. The following quotations about Babel are from Genesis 11v1 – 9.

8. They're talking about building a tower in Saudi Arabia called Kingdom Tower, at *3,280 feet!* That's over a half a mile high.

9. Ecclesiastes 2v17, 20 – 23.

10. An acronym used in this *great* article on Generation Y: Tim Urban, "Why Generation Y Yuppies Are Unhappy," *Huffington Post* (September 15, 2013), http://www.huffingtonpost.com/wait-but-why/generation-y-unhappy_b_3930620.html.

11. I was first exposed to this way of thinking about the good and bad of millennials in Joel Stein's *great* article "The Me Me Me Generation: Why Millennials Will Save Us All," *Time* magazine (May 20, 2013), http://time

.com/247/millennials-the-me-me
-me-generation/.

12. "Africa: Zimbabwe," *The World Factbook*, CIA.gov, https://www.cia.gov/library/publications/the-world-factbook/geos/zi.html.

13. Manel Baucells, Rakesh Sarin, *Engineering Happiness: A New Approach for Building a Joyful Life* (Oakland: University of California Press, 2012), x.

14. I stole this idea from Mike Erre. Actually, I've stolen a lot of ideas from him. Thanks buddy.

I am not a machine

1. Abraham Joshua Heschel, *The Sabbath: Its Meaning for the Modern Man* (New York: Farrar, Straus & Giroux, 1951). Read it! Just once is probably fine.

2. Genesis 2v1–2.

3. I love this prayer from Psalm 90v17.

4. Genesis 2v3.

5. Heschel, *Sabbath*, 8.

6. Exodus 16v23.

7. In John 19v31, the day before the Sabbath is called "the day of Preparation."

8. This part is all from Exodus 20v8–11.

9. Which, by the way, does not mean it's invalid.

10. Exodus 16v29.

11. Romans 14v5.

The anti-Pharaoh

1. The language of "two Torahs" is my own. The word *Torah* is a bit ambiguous. Sometimes it's used for the entire Pentateuch — Genesis through *Deuteronomy*, but then other times (I'm thinking of the writer Paul here) it's used just to mean the Mosaic code starting in Exodus 20 and running forward to *Numbers*. Either way, *Deuteronomy* is very much a "second Torah." It's Moses reiterating the Torah to the *next* generation, forty years after their parents mucked everything up. It can be very interesting to see the similarities and differences between the two. That's all I'm getting at here.

2. To be more precise, that's when it's set. Scholars don't agree on when it was written.

3. This is found in Exodus 20v8–10 and in Deuteronomy 5v12–14. Technically, one word is different. In *Exodus* the first word is "Remember," and in *Deuteronomy* it's "Observe."

4. Exodus 20v11; Deuteronomy 5v15.

5. Exodus 5v4.

6. Exodus 5v5.

7. Exodus 5v9.

8. Exodus 5v10–11.

9. Exodus 5v13.

10. Exodus 5v17–18.

11. Exodus 1v11. Named after the pharaohs not surprisingly.

12. Mark J. Perry, "America's Ridiculously Large $16 Trillion Economy," *American Enterprise Institute* (February 8, 2014), https://www.aei.org/publica tion/americas-ridiculously -large-16-trillion-economy/print/.

13. Ibid.

14. Ibid.

15. Ibid.

16. Ibid.

17. Heschel, *Sabbath*, 3. Once again, read it! So good. This language, actually, this entire chapter, was inspired by *Sabbath as Resistance: Saying No to the Culture of Now* by Walter Brueggemann (Louisville: Westminster John Knox, 2014). Stunning read. Pick it up to learn more.

18. YHWH are the Hebrew letters behind the English translation "the Lord." In English it sounds like a title, but in Hebrew it's a proper name.

The Lord of the Sabbath

1. This story is from Mark 2v23–3v6 NIVUK.

2. Once again, Exodus 20v8–11.

3. John 19v14.

4. This is just Matthew 11v28–30 in *The Message*. So fun to read.

5. Bruggemann, *Sabbath as Resistance*, 43.

Life after heaven

1. 2 Peter 3v10.
2. 2 Peter 3v13.
3. Joel 2v31 KJV.
4. Isaiah 65v17–18, 21–23, emphasis added. Read the rest of the passage. It's stunning.
5. Isaiah 25v6.
6. Joel 3v18.
7. Amos 9v13–14.
8. Isaiah 25v7–8.
9. N. T. Wright in *Surprised by Hope* and a bunch of other places.
10. See Philippians 1v23 and 2 Corinthians 5v8.
11. That's from Revelation 6v9–11, but the entire glimpse into heaven is Revelation 4–6.
12. Matthew 19v28.
13. 1 Corinthians 6v10 and Acts 13v46.
14. Acts 3v21.
15. 2 Peter 3v13.
16. Revelation 21v1.

The people of the future

1. This is a bit of a steal from Rob Bell's *Love Wins: A Book about Heaven, Hell, and the Fate of Every Person Who Ever Lived* (San Francisco: Harper-One, 2011). I don't endorse that book by any stretch, but his chapter on heaven is superb (aside from the fact that he calls the future "heaven," which the biblical authors never do).
2. 1 Corinthians 15v58.
3. Revelation 1v6.
4. Revelation 3v21.
5. Revelation 5v10 ESV.
6. Revelation 20v6.
7. Revelation 22v5.
8. 2 Timothy 2v12.
9. Revelation 14v13.
10. Revelation 21v24, 26.
11. From Miroslav Volf, *Work in the Spirit: Toward a Theology of Work* (Eugene, Ore.: Wipf & Stock, 2001), 91.
12. 1 Corinthians 3v10, 12–15, emphasis added.
13. This is from N. T. Wright's

Surprised by Hope, 193. This is hands down the best book on eschatology I've ever read. In fact, one of the best books on *anything* I've ever read. It honestly changed my life. Go read it!! (Double exclamation points for emphasis.)

14. This is all from Luke 19, emphasis added.

15. Colossians 3v23–24.

16. Alex Ross, "Revelations: The Story behind Messiaen's 'Quartet for the End of Time,'" *The New Yorker* (March 22, 2004), http://www.newyorker.com/archive/2004/03/22/040322crmu_music?currentPage=all.

17. If you want to know more, read Rebecca Rischin's *For the End of Time: The Story of the Messiaen Quartet* (Ithaca, N.Y.: Cornell University Press, 2006).

18. 2 Corinthians 5v17, emphasis added.

Epilogue: Redefining greatness

1. From the article by Lynn Hirshberg, "The Misfit," *Vanity Fair* 54, no. 4 (April 1991); 160–69, 196–202.

2. This is from Mark 9v34, and the rest of the story is from the following paragraph.

3. Plato, *Gorgias*, 491e.

4. That allusion is to 1 Timothy 6v19. Such a great way of putting it.

5. Mark 9v36–37.

6. Such a great term. The article is by Joseph Epstein, "The Kindergarchy: Every Child a Dauphin," *The Weekly Standard*, 13, no. 37 (June 9, 2008): http://www.weeklystandard.com/Content/Public/Articles/000/000/015/161yutrk.asp.

Thanks

Jesus, for letting us rule the world alongside you.

Tammy, Jude, Moses, and Sunday, for Blue Star mornings, Star Wars nights, and life together. Love you so much it hurts.

My parents, for teaching me to dream.

My MC family, for showing me what I never had, and always needed. Fullers, your house this Tuesday?

Matt Norman, for sticking closer than a brother.

Dr. Gerry Breshears, for reading first drafts, and loving me anyways.

N. T. Wright, for reteaching me how to read the entire Bible. And for breakfast in San Francisco. I'm still thinking about that conversation.

Bridgetown Church, where do I even start? I still can't believe I get to do this with you. *In Portland as it is in heaven.*

The Bridgetown staff — Gerald, Deanna, Bethany, Alex,

Salzy, Matt, Travis, Patrick, Justin, Josh, and Tyler — I love you guys like family.

Everybody at Zondervan — Carolyn, David, Tom, Jennifer, Kait, Becky, Joe, Merideth, Paige, you guys have been amazing. And that dinner in Nashville was superb.

All the teachers and writers who shaped this book — N. T. Wright, Chris Wright, Dallas Willard, Tim Keller, Ben Witherington, Abraham Joshua Heschel, Walter Brueggemann, Gerry Breshears, Richard Middleton, and more. I doubt I've ever had an original thought. My goal is just to spread your work as wide as I can. Hopefully, I make you proud.

John Mark Comer lives, works, and writes in the urban core of Portland, Oregon, with his wife, Tammy, and their three children, Jude, Moses, and Sunday.

He is the pastor for teaching and vision at Bridgetown Church, which is part of a family of churches in Portland.

Before planting Bridgetown, John Mark was the college pastor at a megachurch and played in a band. John Mark has a master's degree in biblical and theological studies from Western Seminary and is the author of *Loveology* and *My Name is Hope*.

For more of John Mark's teachings on the Scriptures, Jesus, and life, go to *bridgetownajc.org* and sign up for the podcast or visit *www.johnmarkcomer.com*.